This book is a children's wonderland of stories, picture-puzzles, easy-to-make toys, comic strips, music, and a host of other interesting and exciting things; in fact, turning the pages is like opening a giant Christmas stocking!
It has been created and designed to keep children occupied from that early morning moment when the cry is: "What can I do?" to the evening when a tired voice plaintively asks: "Read me a bedtime story, please."
The original stories are not just absorbing reading but are designed to inspire and encourage children to further activities—they are truly "read-and-do" stories. In addition, there are the much-loved fairy stories which children never tire of reading.
Clearly, this is a book for every day and all day, and one which will appeal also to children who can read and like to use their hands.
The games and activities in this book cover a wide range of interests from simple paper-folding to making a toy town out of boxes. The book, then, is not simply to entertain but to instruct as well. Further, the games and activities are in every way safe, so they need a minimum of parental supervision.

My All Day
Read and Play
Book

Edited by Mary Parsley

American Heritage Press · New York

Designed and produced for the Publisher
by Eurobook Limited, London.

Copyright © 1971 by Eurobook Limited.
Published in 1972 by American Heritage Press,
a division of McGraw-Hill Book Company.

Library of Congress Catalog Card Number: 71-39154

SBN: 07–038831–8

Library Edition SBN 07-038833-4

Printed in Holland

Contents

the daisy chain

You will need: spinner (see page 156), a total of 69 colored markers (these can be cut from colored paper): the number of different colors depends on the number of players. The object of this game is to see who can pick the most daisies for the longest daisy chain. Taking turns, each player spins the spinner: the number he gets is the number of daisies he can "pick," so he covers that number of daisies with his markers. When all the daisies are covered the game is over. Then the markers are counted and the person who covered the most daisies wins the game.

Bertha and the Television

Bertha loved watching television, especially if there were horses in the show. She liked show jumping, racing, and parades with soldiers on horses. Her very very favorite films were stories of the wild west.

Bertha didn't have a television set of her own. She always went to William's house to watch it. You see, Bertha was a horse herself. She belonged to William and lived on his farm.

Mrs. William didn't want Bertha trampling round in the house. So Bertha stood outside, and watched through the window.

One day, she watched her big western hero, Cowboy Joe, and his beautiful horse Gloria. They had a super adventure, and Bertha loved it. But she got so excited she forgot where she was standing, and trampled on the flowers by the window.

Mrs. William was very angry when she found out. She wouldn't let Bertha come to the house any more. Bertha was very sad. She moped all day, and even more at night, when the television was on.

One morning William told her, "Cowboy Joe was on television last night. He said that his horse, Gloria, is retiring. He's looking for a new horse to go on television with him. Would you like to try out for the part?"

"Oh, yes!" cried Bertha, feeling quite giddy at the thought of perhaps meeting her handsome hero, Cowboy Joe.

So William took her to the studios. They met Cowboy Joe, and he went for a ride on Bertha's back.

"You're just the horse I've been looking for!" he told her. "Will you be mine?"

Bertha said yes, though she was almost fainting with joy. But she managed not to – which was just as well, for Cowboy Joe was still on her back at the time!

So she became Cowboy Joe's horse. Every day they galloped about, having adventures and being filmed for television.

And every night Bertha watched herself on television. She had her very own set, right in her stall in the stable.

Make your own Television

You will need: small cardboard box with lid, 2 long pencils – at least 1 inch longer than the box is wide, 2 wooden spools, paper – strong but thin, strong glue, sticky tape

1. Measure the width of your box. Now make a strip of paper 4 feet long and 2 inches narrower than the box.

2. Draw pictures all along the paper strip.

3. Using sticky tape, fasten the ends of the strip to the pencils – the same way a flag is fastened to a stick.

4. Remove the lid of the box and set it aside. Stand the box on one of its long sides. This side is now the bottom of the TV set. Inside the bottom – about $\frac{1}{2}$ inch from one side and $\frac{3}{4}$ inch from the front, glue a wooden spool. Glue another spool in the matching spot by the other side.

5. Working from the outside, make two small holes in what is now the top of the box. These holes must be straight above the spools and just big enough to push the pencils through.

6. Fit the pencils – with the strip of paper fastened between them – into the box. This is done from the inside of the box. Push the pencil tops through the holes in the top, until the paper strip touches the top of the box. Then slip the other ends of the pencils into the holes in the spools.

7. Cut a hole, shaped like a television screen, in the center of the lid. Leave a frame of 1 inch at top, 2 inches at bottom of the screen, and $1\frac{1}{2}$ inches at each side. Put the lid on the box, and your television is ready for viewing. To make the pictures move, hold one pencil by its top, where it sticks out of the box top. Wind it around – and the pictures move across the screen.

The Lost Pets

Mr. Snuffit, the pet store owner, stands in the street looking very puzzled. He's trying to find fifteen pets that have escaped from his store. Can you help him?

(See page 156 for the answers)

Fruit Salad

You will need: one banana, two oranges, one apple, one pear, one small can of pineapple chunks or rings. Blunt knife, orange squeezer, large bowl

1. Peel a banana, slice it with the knife, and put it in a bowl.
2. Peel one of the oranges by cutting through the thick orange peel like this:
First around one way.
Then around the other way.
Then peel back each of the sections of skin. Peel away as much of the thin white skin as you can. Divide the orange into segments and add to the banana in the bowl.
3. Quarter an apple and then cut out its core. Ask someone to help if you have trouble doing this.
Now cut the apple into pieces and add to the bowl.
4. Quarter a pear, and cut out its core. Cut in half again and then cut these into small pieces. (You can use canned pears instead.)
5. Ask someone to help you open a small can of pineapple. If the pineapple is in chunks, add these to the bowl of fruit.
If it is in rings, cut them into pieces before adding.
6. Cut the second orange in half, squeeze the juice, and add the juice to the fruit.
7. If you have some cherries, take out the stones and add them. Now serve the fruit salad in a big bowl. It will make a delicious dessert.

14

A Pomander

Here's a very simple present to make. It is called a pomander, and when it is hung in a closet it makes everything smell sweet.
You will need: a thin-skinned orange, a box of cloves, ribbon (about $\frac{1}{4}$ or $\frac{1}{2}$ inch wide)

1. Mark two bands around the orange, like this, where the ribbon will go. Make sure the bands are the same width as the ribbon.
2. Stick cloves all over the orange – except in these bands.
3. Store the orange in a warm, dry place for about a month (until it is dry and hard).
4. Wrap the ribbon around in the bands, where there are no cloves. Wrap one length of ribbon one way, and fasten with glue. Then wrap another strip the other way and fasten.

Now you have a special Christmas or birthday present for a friend.

Cranberry Garlands

You may have eaten cranberry sauce with turkey, but did you know that cranberries can be used for Christmas tree decoration?
You will need: one box of cranberries, needle, thread

1. Thread a needle with a long, strong thread. Tie a good knot at the end.
2. String the cranberries on the thread, as if they were beads. Cranberries are not juicy, so there won't be a mess.
3. When you have the thread nearly full of cranberries, take the needle off and tie a knot in the end.
4. Then start again with another thread. String as many threads as you need, until all the cranberries are gone. Then tie the strings together to make one very long and beautiful string of berry-beads.
5. Drape the string over the Christmas tree. To make a lovely red-and-white garland, you can use popcorn, too. String one piece of popcorn, then two cranberries, then another piece of popcorn, and so on.

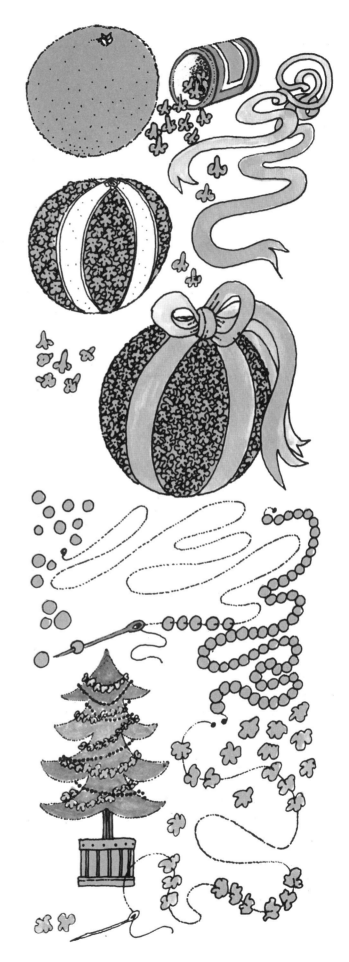

Fables from Aesop
Town Mouse and Country Mouse

A town mouse went to visit his country cousin for dinner. But he didn't enjoy his food, which was just some muddy roots from the field.

"Your food is terrible," said the town mouse, "and so is your muddy hole in the ground. You should come and see how I live in the town."

They went to the town mouse's home, which was in a rich man's larder. There was plenty of rich food, but they couldn't get to it. The cat frightened them away.

The country mouse left the house. "You can keep your fine food," he said. "I'd rather live in my poor muddy hole, where it is safe and quiet."

The Boy Who Cried Wolf

A shepherd boy liked playing jokes on people. Several times he rushed into town, shouting: "Help! Help! A wolf is eating my sheep!"

Each time he cried "Wolf!" the people rushed to help him. But they never found a wolf. "Ha, ha!" laughed the boy. "I fooled you again!"

One day a wolf really did attack the sheep. The boy rushed to town for help. But everyone laughed at him: "You can't catch us with that old trick!"

So the wolf took all the boy's sheep. And the moral of the tale is this:
People won't believe a liar, even when he tells the truth.

John and His Ball

John went out to play with his new ball. He walked along the road, rolling it in front of him.

He had not gone far when he met a farmer.

"Hello," said the farmer. "That's a nice ball."

"Yes," said John. "My daddy gave it to me."

"My dog would love a ball," said the farmer. "Will you give it to me, if I give you some apples?"

John liked the farmer's dog, so he said "Yes." The farmer gave him a bag of apples.

John went on down the road.

"What are you doing with those apples?" another boy called from his garden.

"A farmer gave them to me," said John.

"Will you give me some, if I show you my new train set?" said the other boy.

"Oh, yes," said John. The other boy ran
indoors. He came back with his train set. They
had a game with it on the grass until tea-time.

"I must go now," said John. "My father
comes home soon. I hope he won't be cross
because I gave away my ball."

"I've got lots of balls," said the other boy.
"I'll give you one. After all, you did give me a
very big bag of apples."

"Oh, thank you," said John.

"Come and play another day," said the boy.

"I'll come soon," said John. "Goodbye!"

He ran home with his new ball.

Sylvia's Tricycle

A handsome tricycle – whose name was Trike – was made in a factory. From there Trike went to a shop. A man bought him, and took him home.

The man gave Trike to his little daughter, Sylvia. She loved Trike, for he was the best toy she'd ever had. She rode him up and down the path in front of her house, showing him off. She wanted everyone to see how smart he looked. He had glittery silver spokes that winked in the sun when his wheels moved. He was painted bright red, with fancy gold lines on top. He did look fine.

Then Sylvia bumped Trike into the gate, and scratched his paint. "Oooo, that hurts!" he cried. But she didn't hear him, for who ever heard a tricycle talking?

Her father saw the scratch, though. "You should take care of Trike," he said. "He won't look so smart if you keep knocking him into things."

Sylvia was sorry then. So, for a while, she took good care of Trike, and didn't scratch him. But soon she forgot. She bumped Trike into lots of things. Before long he was scratched and dented all over. A few parts grew loose, and he began to rattle. Sometimes Trike was left out in the rain. He started to rust.

Sylvia didn't notice. Trike was her favorite toy, and she played with him every day. But she never really looked at him, to see how he was.

Then, one day, she rode Trike straight into a tree. She didn't mean to hurt him, but she was so busy playing, she forgot to take care. Crunch! Trike's big front wheel was bent when it hit the tree.

Sylvia tried to ride him, but his wheel wobbled. He was very hard to steer. She had to walk home, pulling poor wobbly Trike behind her.

Just as they reached her house, down came the rain. Sylvia ran indoors, leaving Trike out on the lawn, soaking wet. He stayed there all the rest of the day. When night came, he was still there.

Trike was very unhappy. His front wheel was hurting, too. "She's treated me too badly this time," he thought. "I shall run away, tonight, before she ruins me!"

So he crept off, in the rainy dark – rattle, *skwonk*, clunk! He *was* battered, poor little fellow.

Soon he was very weary, for it was hard

work trying to move with a bent wheel. He came to a dark alley and hid there while he had a rest.

Trike was so tired that he fell asleep, leaning against a trash can. He didn't wake up until the morning, when he felt someone pick him up.

It was the junk man! "I guess Sylvia's thrown away this old tricycle," he said. "I'll take it to break up for scrap."

Clang! He threw Trike on to his cart, which was full of old metal. Then he drove the cart up the road.

Poor Trike wept oily tears to himself. "This is the end of me," he cried.

The junk cart went past Sylvia's house. She was outside, looking for Trike, and she saw him on the cart.

"That's my Trike!" she shouted to the junk man. "Please, can I have him back?"

"Certainly," said the junk man. He took Trike from the cart and gave him to Sylvia. "You should take better care of your toys," he told her. "Your tricycle is so battered, he looked just like old junk to me!"

Trike was very, very happy to be home again. Sylvia was happy to have him back, but she was also sorry about the state he was in. So she took Trike to her father, and asked him to help.

Sylvia's father took Trike to pieces. He straightened out the bends and dents, and covered him with bright new paint. When the paint was dry, he put Trike together again, and oiled all his squeaky parts.

From that day on, Sylvia took good care of him. She didn't scratch or dent him, or leave him out in the rain.

Trike was happy ever after, and he never wanted to run away again.

FRÈRE JACQUES

Frè-re Jac-ques,   Frè-re Jac-ques,   Dor-mez vous?   Dor-mez vous?
Broth-er John,   Broth-er John,   Are you sleep-ing? Are you sleep-ing?

Son-nez les ma-ti-nes, Son-nez les ma-ti-nes: Din Din Don Din Din Don
Morn-ing bells are ringing, Morn-ing bells are ringing: Ding Ding Dong Ding Ding Dong

Emma's Elephant

Emma had lots of toys but the one she loved best was Tweekle, her elephant. She had made up his name all by herself. He had only a little trunk, because he wasn't very old, but his ears were big and floppy. He wasn't dark grey like the elephants Emma had seen at the zoo. Tweekle was a pretty color, but when Emma was drawing a picture of him she couldn't find a crayon in her box which was the same color. Her mother showed her that if she used a blue crayon and then a pink crayon on top she would get the right color. Mother said, "When summer comes the lilac trees in the garden will be in flower, and you will see that they are the same color as Tweekle."

Tweekle had big, wide-open eyes, and he looked as if he were listening to everything Emma said. His eyes were always open, even in bed. When Emma went to sleep he didn't shut his eyes. Mother said this was because he was watching over Emma all night. Emma often talked to Tweekle.

"I would never let you go to the zoo, Tweekle," she said, "and give children rides on your back. Daddy says elephants have to lift heavy trees with their trunks. I wouldn't let you do that either. You must always stay here and play with me."

One day Emma went shopping with her mother. Tweekle went too, because he went everywhere with Emma, and sat next to her in the car. He had even been in an airplane when it was time for vacation. Mother had a lot of things to buy, but at last she

was ready to go home. Emma climbed into the car, and Mother drove off. When they came to their house, Emma wanted to get out of the car quickly, but when she turned around, Tweekle wasn't there!

"Mother, I can't find Tweekle!" she cried.

Mother helped her look for him, but they couldn't find him anywhere. He was not in the car!

Emma began to cry. "Oh dear! He's lost!"

"Don't cry," said Mother. "We'll go back to the shops. You must have left him there." Everyone at the shops knew Tweekle. They had often seen him with Emma.

Mrs. Figg in the fruit-shop shook her head. She was very sorry, but he wasn't there. Mr. Bull, the butcher, hadn't seen him; and he wasn't in the paper shop, although Emma looked behind the big bundles of newspapers in case he was hiding. She began to sob once more. Suppose she never saw Tweekle again? What if another child had him? He would be very sad without her. She was sure of that. How could she go to bed without Tweekle? What if she woke in the dark and he wasn't there with his head on the pillow beside her and his eyes wide open?

"We'll ask Mr. Gingerbread," said Mother. Mr. Gingerbread was the baker. He was a fat, jolly man and he laughed a lot, but today he was not laughing. He had not seen Tweekle either. Just then the bell above the door tinkled – tring! tring! – and a little boy and his mother came into the shop. The boy was holding a toy rabbit in one arm and in the other arm he was holding – can you guess?

Emma stopped crying just as if she had turned off her tears like a water tap. She rushed at the little boy and pulled Tweekle out of his arms.

"Emma, remember your manners!" said Mother. Emma looked at the boy. She had seen him before. He had just come to live in a house on her road.

"What's your name?" she asked.

"Simon," said the little boy.

"What's your rabbit's name?"

"Cottontail," said Simon. His rabbit had a little red jacket and a white tail.

Simon's mother was telling Emma's mother how Simon had seen Tweekle fall out of the car when Emma climbed in and how they were going to stop at her house on their way and give Tweekle back to her.

Emma was so happy to have Tweekle back that she wasn't really listening to them, but then she heard her mother saying, "Simon and his mother are coming to tea tomorrow. Won't that be nice? Now you've made a new little friend."

"Tweekle has made a new friend, too," said Emma. "His friend is called Cottontail."

Sleeping Beauty

Once upon a time, there lived a king and queen whose lives were perfect – except for one thing. For many years they had no child. Finally, however, the queen gave birth to a beautiful baby daughter.

The king and queen were delighted, and they held an enormous banquet to celebrate. They invited hundreds of guests, including seven fairies who were to be godmothers to the little girl and give her magic presents like beauty, grace, goodness, and so on.

There had never been a banquet like it. Gold plates, knives, forks, and spoons were set at every place, and in addition each fairy was given a wonderful golden casket, studded with precious stones.

But just as everyone was sitting down at the table, in stormed another fairy.

The eighth!

But where the others were pretty and good, she was ugly, and very, very bad.

"What's the meaning of not inviting me?" she screamed. "Me, the oldest and most powerful of all the fairies! Lay a place for me immediately."

A gold plate, knife, fork, and spoon were soon laid for the Wicked Fairy. But not a golden casket.

"I'm afraid we only had seven made," the king explained.

"If you don't mind waiting we'll send one to you later . . ." added the queen.

But it was no good. The Wicked Fairy was furious, and all through the meal she never stopped muttering to herself about what she would like to do to the king and queen for insulting her.

Now, luckily, one of the other fairies overheard this, and realized she was going to do something bad. So when the meal was finished, the Good Fairy slipped away from the table and hid behind a curtain where no one could see her, but where she could hear everything that went on.

The time came for all the guests to give the baby princess her birthday presents. Some gave gold; some gave silver; some gave precious stones; some gave all three. But the most important presents of all were those of the fairies. One by one they walked to the princess's cradle and blessed her with a magic present.

The first said she would be beautiful. The second that she would be good. The third that she would be kind. And so on, until it was the turn of the Wicked Fairy.

"Hmn, I'll give you something you won't forget in a hurry," she snarled, looking down at the poor baby. "You'll be pretty, and good, and kind and all the rest of it, only one day – and I won't say when – you will prick your finger on a spindle. And then you will die!"

Everyone was horrified, and for a moment there wasn't a sound to be heard in all the great hall.

Then the Good Fairy stepped out from where she had been hiding. "No!" she said. "The princess will NOT die. I haven't given her my blessing yet, and though I can't stop her pricking her finger, I can stop her dying. Instead she will fall asleep – for a hundred years. And at the end of that time a king's son will awaken her."

The princess's parents weren't at all happy at what had happened, but at least they knew their little girl wasn't going to die.

All the same, the king tried to cheat the Wicked Fairy. He made a law that nobody in his kingdom could use a spindle. In fact he had all the spindles collected together and burned on an enormous, blazing fire.

But then, when the princess was fifteen years old, the king and queen went on a visit to a neighboring country. They left the princess behind – they had to, since there were bound to be lots of spindles in a foreign country.

But as it turned out, there was danger at home – in the king's own castle!

One day the princess was playing, running all over the castle from room to room, and in a tiny little room at the top of a tall tower she found an old, old woman who was spinning. With a spindle!

"Please, what are you doing?" the princess asked.

"Why, I'm spinning wool, child," the old woman replied.

"Isn't that against the law?" the princess asked.

"Against the law? Well, I never! Why, I've been sitting in this room spinning wool for fifteen years, and nobody told *me* it was against the law! Would you like to try?"

The princess said yes. She reached out her hand and . . . "OUCH!"

She pricked her finger on the spindle.

Then, quite quietly, she slipped to the floor and lay absolutely still, with her eyes tightly closed.

The old woman ran for help, but there was nothing anyone could do. The princess was sound asleep.

It was at that moment that the king and queen arrived home.

The king ordered that his daughter be carried to the finest room in the castle, and laid on a gold bed covered with silk.

No sooner had this been done when the Good Fairy arrived at the castle. She had really known all along exactly when the princess would prick her finger. And she had come because she also knew how terrible it would be for the princess to awake after a hundred years to find herself among strangers.

So the Good Fairy went all through the castle touching everything and everyone with her magic wand. And as she did they instantly fell fast asleep. The king and queen slept in the throne room, the soldiers on the battlements, the horses in the stables, the fires in the grates, the clocks on the walls . . . even the wind stopped blowing.

Finally, she made a great thick hedge of holly and thorns spring up all around the castle. Higher and higher, thicker and thicker it grew, until not even the tallest towers could be seen.

Slowly the days passed, then the months, and years. The seasons came and went, and came again, and still the princess slept.

Beyond the great thorny hedge, life went on. Nobody ever went near the enchanted castle. The parliament of the country met and made the king's brother king in his place, and soon it was as if the princess, the king and queen, and the castle had never existed at all.

But then a hundred years to the very day after the princess had pricked her finger, the son of the king of that time happened to ride by the great hedge surrounding the castle. He had passed by many times before, but suddenly, and without knowing why, he wanted to know what lay behind the great hedge.

He asked his servants, but they didn't know, so he asked the people living in the neighborhood. At first it seemed as if they didn't know either, but finally an old man approached the prince.

"Your Royal Highness," he said, "I remember, long ago, my own father telling me that when he was a lad a great castle stood here: the king's castle. But a wicked fairy put a curse on the king's daughter, and she fell asleep and the whole castle with her. He said she would sleep for a hundred years."

At that the prince leaped from his horse, and, drawing his sword, rushed at the great wall of prickles.

But instead of his having to cut his way through as he expected, the branches seemed to part before him, only to close again behind him so that none of his servants could follow.

Soon the prince reached the castle courtyard, and then he was inside the castle itself. Everywhere it was the same: people lying sleeping on the ground, leaning against walls, sitting on chairs. But the prince wasn't interested in them. He was looking for the princess. And then he found her – asleep on her great golden bed.

The prince had never seen anyone so lovely in his whole life. He just couldn't help kissing her.

And the moment he did, she opened her eyes and smiled. The spell was broken!

With a crash, the great thorny hedge around the castle tumbled to the ground. Sun came flooding back through the windows. The clocks began to tick again, the fires glowed, and the pots began to bubble. Dogs barked, birds sang, and all over the castle people began to yawn and stretch.

The princess and her prince ran together to the throne room, and the prince asked the king if he could marry the princess. He agreed quickly enough, you can be sure, and soon the old castle echoed with the sounds of a marvelous wedding feast.

It was the most wonderful wedding that anyone ever had – before or since – and this time there was no Bad Fairy to spoil things.

And the prince and princess? Well, they lived happily ever after.

Jack in a Box

You will need: yogurt carton, paper, lightweight cardboard, paint, tracing paper, scissors, knitting wool, box, sticky tape, *used* wooden matchstick

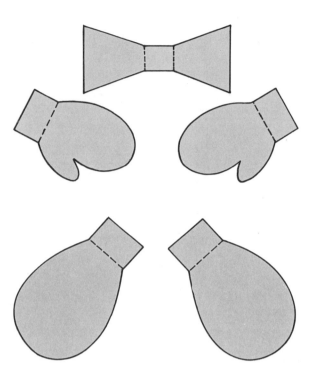

1. First wash the yogurt carton and dry it. Don't worry if your carton isn't the same shape as ours: your Jack will just be a different shape. If your carton is cardboard, it will be easy to cut off the rim with scissors, so that Jack's paper suit will fit better. Put glue all over the carton and wrap a piece of clean paper around it which is taller than the carton. If you've left the rim on, glue the paper up to the rim, but not on it.

3. Trace the hands, feet, and bow shown here onto tracing paper. Now turn the paper over, put it against some lightweight cardboard, and draw over the lines again. Now that the tracing is on the card, paint the shapes and then cut them out. When they are dry bend the flaps where the dotted lines are.
Stick the hands to Jack's sides. The feet flaps should stick onto the bottom of the carton. The bow tie should be folded and the middle of it should be stuck to the top of Jack's shirt.

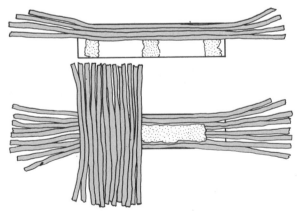

2. Cut off the spare paper at the bottom. Now paint on the face and clothes. Make a belt from a painted strip of paper, and stick it round Jack's middle with glue.

4. To make the wig, cut a strip of paper long enough to stick to either side of the head. Cut lots of lengths of wool. Put glue on the paper and stick the strips of wool down all over the paper.

5. Put glue around the top of Jack's head and press the wig onto the glue. Give him a haircut if you like.

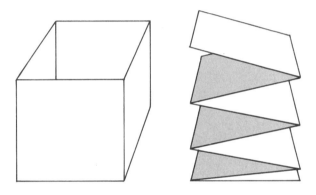

6. Cut a long strip of flexible card (possibly from a cereal box) as wide as Jack's box. Fold it accordion style. This is Jack's spring.

7. Glue the bottom of the carton to the top flap of the spring. Tape the top fold to the second one to make it stand flat. Make sure you have enough folds to make Jack jump right to the top of the box.

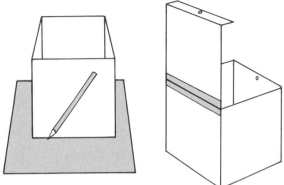

8. To make a lid, draw around the bottom of Jack's box onto some card and add a flap for the front. Cut it out and stick the lid to the box with sticky tape. Tuck the lid down and make a small hole through the front of the box and the flap of the lid. Stick a *used* matchstick through both holes as a fastener. When you want Jack to jump, pull the matchstick out. To decorate the box paint it and then add some painted strips.

CRAZY CAR RACE

You will need: spinner (to make spinner see page 156) and 5 markers made from paper or buttons or something similar. This is a game you can play by yourself or with a friend. The object of the game is to see which car wins the race. Spin the spinner: the number you get is the number of the first car to be passed by all the others. Put a marker on it. Keep spinning until you have put all but one of the cars out of the race. The one that is left uncovered is the winner. On your mark, get set . . . GO!

Mr. Pinktoe and the Imaginary Subject

One evening, Mr. Pinktoe came home from his office very excited. He burst into the kitchen, throwing his briefcase on the floor, where it knocked over the cat's milk. Mrs. Pinktoe was very surprised. Usually Mr. Pinktoe entered the kitchen rather timidly.

"What's all this, then?" she cried, as she put the potatoes on to boil.

"It's a chance to win a prize," replied her husband, his words tumbling out. "A complete artist's kit, to be precise. All you have to do is to paint a picture on any imaginary subject. I've been waiting for a chance like this ever since I painted that picture in the country last summer."

Mrs. Pinktoe knew the picture he meant. She liked it, even though she knew that Mr. Pinktoe had painted in the cows' spots after he got home. But though she had faith in Mr. Pinktoe, she wasn't sure his painting was good enough to win a prize.

But she said, "How lovely."

All through supper, Mr. Pinktoe talked about the competition. Mrs. Pinktoe was waiting to tell him about a broken chair leg, but she had no chance. He kept wondering what he could paint. "An imaginary subject," it had said. Noah's Ark? No, he'd had enough trouble with painting a few cows; he'd never manage a giraffe. Fairies, then? No, not that either. He could never work out how their wings fitted onto their backs. He wandered round the room, wondering. Just as he passed the bookcase, the answer came to him – Robin Hood!

Ever since Mr. Pinktoe had learned to read, his hero had been Robin Hood. In the bookcase were dozens of Robin Hood books, which he had read dozens of times.

Every evening Mr. Pinktoe gobbled down his supper, and took out his painting gear. Robin Hood, Friar Tuck, Maid Marion—he even dreamed about them. On Saturday, though, his wife managed to ask him about mending the chair. As he walked down to the tool shed, his neighbor, Mr. Ivor Ffinger-Greene, popped his head over the fence.

"Busy, Mr. Pinktoe?"

"Just going to mend a chair," answered Mr. Pinktoe. "But what's really keeping me busy is my picture. I'm going in for a competition."

Mr. Ffinger-Greene leaned further over the fence.

"Oh, I know. Your wife told my wife. Robin Hood, eh? I must say, I thought he was only for children, like Santa Claus. Ha, ha! As a matter of fact," he added, with a smirk, "I'm going in for the competition, too. I dabble in oils, you know. But my subject's a secret."

It wasn't a secret for long. Later on, Mr. Pinktoe heard Mr. Ffinger-Greene and his wife in their garden.

He crept inquisitively up to the fence and peered through a knot hole. Mr. Ffinger-Greene had set up his easel on the lawn, and

Mrs. Ffinger-Greene, dressed in nothing but two old sheepskin rugs from the bedroom, was striking a rather chilly pose.

"Must be something prehistoric," guessed Mr. Pinktoe. "I'll have to look to my laurels."

He didn't need models. In his mind, he knew exactly how Robin and his men should look. He spent a long time mixing his Lincoln Green and a nice gray stone color for Nottingham Castle. Little John was his biggest problem. If he drew him too tall, all the other Merry Men looked like gnomes. If he made him too small, he looked just like an ordinary Merry Man.

Competition day was nearly upon him. He worked harder than ever, and even made himself late for the office. But at last, on the very morning of the competition day, his masterpiece was finished. He put in the final brush-stroke just before lunch. It was a nuisance that the picture was still wet.

"Perhaps if I leave it outside while I have my lunch," he thought, "it will be dry and ready for the selection this afternoon."

He leaned the picture carefully against the garden fence, took one last satisfied glance, and went in to lunch.

Unknown to Mr. Pinktoe, Mr. Ffinger-Greene was peeping through the knot hole. He had been waiting for an opportunity to spoil Mr. Pinktoe's chances, and this was it! Paints in hand, he tiptoed round to Mr. Pinktoe's garden, and tampered with the scene of Robin Hood. "Pinktoe will be a laughing stock!" he leered. Mr. Pinktoe, meanwhile, had finished his lunch and was checking that his entry form was properly filled in. One sentence gave him a horrid shock. "Pictures to be submitted by 2 p.m." Mr. Pinktoe had thought it was 2:30! It was nearly two o'clock now!

Rushing out, he flung a big sheet of brown paper over his picture, without looking at it, and ran all the way to the hall.

He was just in time. Mr. Ffinger-Greene was already there, grinning in anticipation of his award.

"Pinktoe hasn't a ghost of a chance now!" he chuckled to himself.

How wrong he was! As Mr. Pinktoe unwrapped his picture in front of the judge, they both stared at it, Mr. Pinktoe in horror, and the judge in ecstasy.

"This work of art shows more imagination than anything I've ever seen!" declared the judge. "Mr. Pinktoe – the prize is yours!"

Mr. Pinktoe's picture had won the competition on the strength of Mr. Ffinger-Greene's interfering alterations. Mr. Pinktoe knew what the changes were – and so did Mr. Ffinger-Greene, who was sulking in a corner. But do you know what they were? Turn the page and look at Mr. Pinktoe's picture – and see if you can guess!

MAKE SOMETHING SIMPLE
paper plane

You will need: a *square* of stiff paper

1. Fold the paper in half to find the middle and open out flat. Fold the top corners down into the middle (A), and fold in half (B).

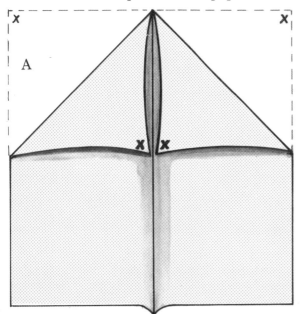

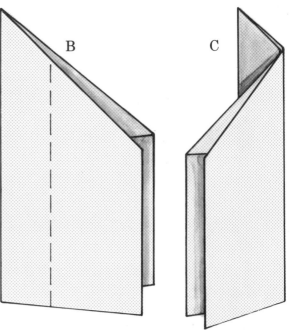

2. Make a crease down the paper on the dotted line (B), and fold the paper over (C).

3. Now open out the top piece and press flat so that it looks like picture (D).

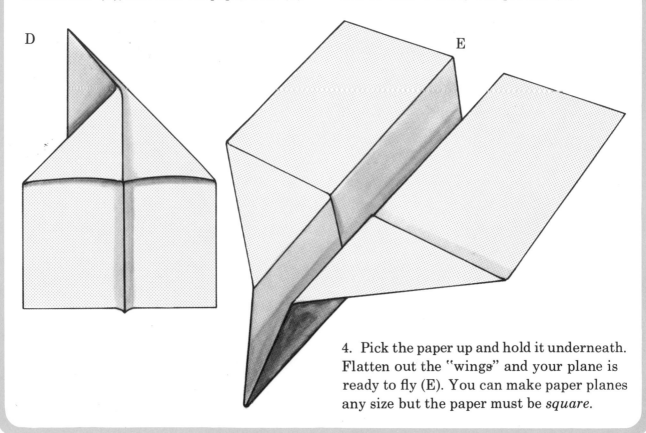

4. Pick the paper up and hold it underneath. Flatten out the "wings" and your plane is ready to fly (E). You can make paper planes any size but the paper must be *square*.

paper snake

1. Cut a long, thin strip of paper and fold it in half. Color one side. Now mark in the lines like the ones in the picture.

2. Fold down the first line and press the paper flat. This is the snake's nose.

3. Now fold along the second line upwards so that the white side shows.

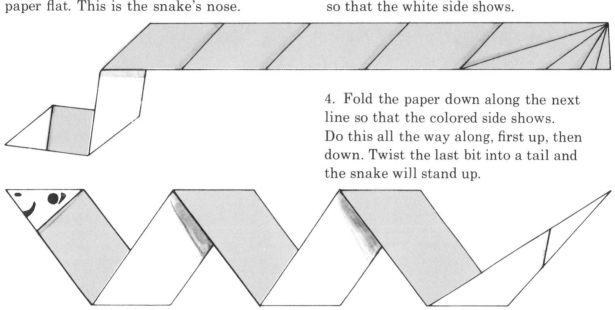

4. Fold the paper down along the next line so that the colored side shows. Do this all the way along, first up, then down. Twist the last bit into a tail and the snake will stand up.

cut-out dolls

1. Cut a long strip of paper and measure it off into squares. Then fold it up.

2. Draw a little figure on the top square with her arms out to the edges of the paper. Cut around your figure but be sure not to cut across her hands. Now open the paper out and there are your dolls.

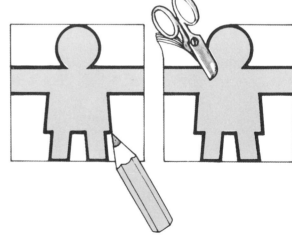

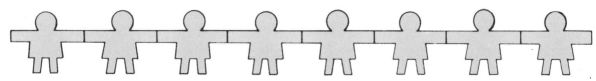

Decorating Eggs

What's more fun than an Easter egg hunt? Decorating the eggs, of course! Here's how to do it.

You will need: hard-boiled eggs, several different food colorings or special egg dyes, cups or bowls, tablespoons, apron

1. Make sure the eggs are hard-boiled. They must be boiled for 10-15 minutes. Mother will be happy to do this for you.

3. Mix each color in a different cup.

5. To make patterned eggs, first decorate the egg with crayons. Draw flowers, stripes, polka dots, or any design you like. You could even write your name on one of them. Dip the egg into a dye that looks good with the color of the crayon-pattern.

2. To dye the eggs, use different food colorings (or special Easter egg dyes), which can be bought from a grocer. Wear an apron, and be extra-careful not to splash the dyes.

4. Now, using a spoon, put each egg into a bowl of dye. If you want a pale color leave the egg in the dye for just a few seconds. The darker the color you want, the longer the egg should be left in.

6. You can decorate eggs with water colors, or with felt pens. But if you use food coloring or special egg dyes, it will be completely safe to eat the eggs later.

Toad's Triumph

As always, the animals were holding their Annual Sports on Midsummer Day. It was the only day of the year (except Christmas Day, when most of them were asleep anyway) that they all gathered together peacefully. The song thrushes promised not to eat the snails, and the badger gave his word that he would not be tempted by the young rabbits. No one trusted the fox, however, so he wasn't invited.

Each animal had his own favorite sporting event, and had been practicing for weeks in advance. The actual day held few surprises. Though the moles cherished a secret ambition to win the long jump, they could never steal a march on the hares. The rabbits would have given their ears to throw the furthest, but they were always defeated by the squirrels. Little did anyone know that every squirrel was in collusion with a nuthatch, who caught the nut in his

beak as the squirrel threw it, and flew several hundred yards with it, breaking records each year. They shared the prize.

There was only one animal who scored very little success in any sport – the toad. He always complained bitterly that there were no underwater events, for he was so much more nimble-footed in water than on dry land. He was so tremendously eager to be a champion that this year he had taken steps which would bring him certain glory. Early in the morning of the Sports Day, the toad disappeared . . .

Punctually at two o'clock, all the suitably clad competitors and spectators assembled in Farmer Beet's largest meadow. Occupying a table at one end of the field was the chief judge, the badger. He looked very imposing under a layer of cast-off sweaters, with his stop-watch at his elbow. Three sharp-eyed jackdaws guarded the trophies, and the dormouse, who was very literate, was appointed as recorder of speeds and distances.

Gradually the excited animals were brought into some sort of order by the stoat stewards.

"Into position all competitors for the flat race," announced the woodpecker.

Several long-legged hares crouched in position, whiskers twitching in anticipation. Just as the woodpecker was about to tap his beak sharply for the start, a hedgehog boldly joined the line-up. Noticing that the course was downhill, he had decided to try his luck by curling up tightly and rolling very fast. Cheered on and whistled at, they leaped off, the swift hares soon out-distancing the little hedgehog. But the winning hare, who owed his success to a very careful diet during training, insisted upon shaking the hedgehog's paw, as a sign of respect.

As everyone had expected, the grasshoppers had no competition in the high jump.

"They're too cocky by far, those grasshoppers," muttered the moles. "Listen to them applaud themselves with their back legs all the time."

The obstacle race was a fairer fight, for it involved a mixture of tunneling, running, and jumping. The caterpillars, arching and twisting, tore down the track on the double, finally curling themselves triumphantly round the winning tape.

The moles, snails, and frogs had fought two very close finishes in the egg-and-spoon and the sack races before anyone noticed that the toad was missing. This was a cause of great anxiety. The rabbit competitors for the hurdles waited on tenterhooks, wondering whether to begin or to join in the hunt for the toad. After half an hour's futile search, everyone was hot and tired.

Suddenly, from the outskirts of the wood, came the unfamiliar noise of a tinkle and a clatter. Everyone turned, and goggled. Pedaling laboriously up the incline, puffing hard but beaming, was the missing toad. From goodness-knew-where, he had obtained a bicycle and ice cream cart. Attached to the back of the cart was a garish sign which read, "T. Toad. Finest Flavored Ice Creams," embellished with a flourish.

Toad was soon surrounded by a joyful throng. It was for this moment of glory that he had labored the whole morning, mixing up the most mouth-watering ice creams— parsley, carrot-top, lettuce, hazelnut, honeysuckle and dandelion. Everyone's taste had been catered to. But Toad refused to reveal where he had borrowed the cart and bicycle and merely said that they had better eat up quickly, for he had to return the gear by six o'clock.

When the trays were quite empty, the badger, wiping his snout carefully, held up a paw for silence.

"Toad," he said, "on behalf of all animals present, I wish to thank you for your delicious refreshments. And," he continued, "it has been suggested to me that in your honor, a special race should take place, to wit, a Bicycle Race! Competitors for this event, line up, please!"

At last Toad had his prize. For in that race he was, of course, the only competitor!

Making Mosaics

There are many things that can be used to make mosaic pictures, decorations, and jewelry. Those listed here are just a few, but you may be able to think of others. If you like, paint pasta and rice and let it dry before using it. You will probably think of all sorts of different things to make from these.

You will need: various seeds, pasta, rice, coffee beans, pretty buttons, dried leaves and flowers, glue, paper or cardboard

1. To make a pretty pin, cut the shape you want from heavy cardboard.

2. Spread glue all over the cardboard. Now fix the seeds, buttons, pasta, etc., to the card, making an interesting pattern.

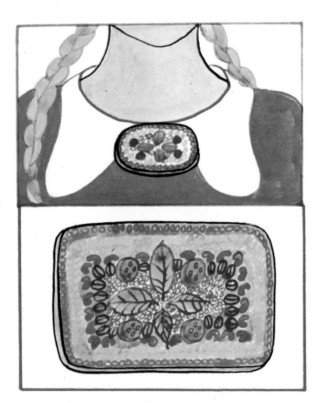

Now you have a pretty pin to wear, or to give to someone as a present.

You can also make a simple mosaic picture. Draw the picture with pencil first, then trace the lines with glue. Then fix the bits and pieces into place.

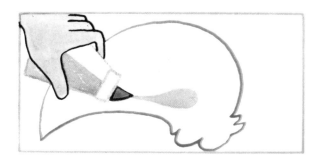

2. Spread glue on the picture, a little at a time, so that it doesn't dry before you get the bits and pieces down.

1. Draw a big picture of a hen.

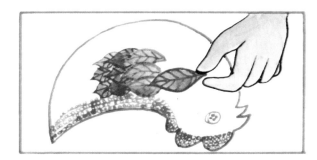

3. Use a button for the hen's eye, coffee beans for her head and breast, dried leaves for her wings, golden lentils or dried corn for her beak and eggs, and painted pasta and rice to fill in the rest.

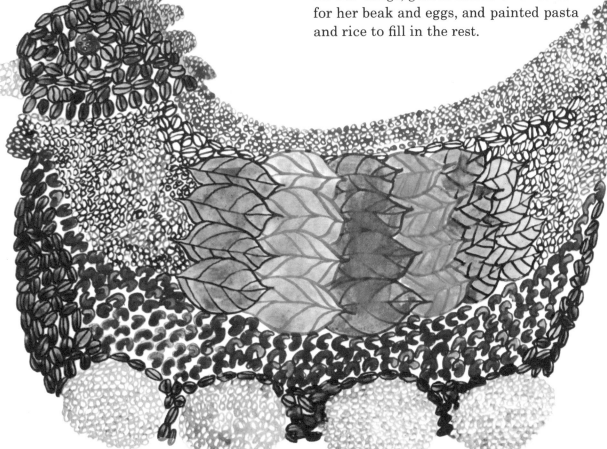

The Fabulous Hippopotamus

Young Andrew was covered all over in bright red spots, and he didn't feel very well. So his mother put him to bed and called the doctor.

"You've got measles," said the doctor when he saw Andrew. "You must stay in bed till they go away again."

For two days Andrew didn't mind staying in bed, for he really felt ill. But soon he began to feel better. He wanted to get out of bed.

"No, you must stay there for a few more days," said his mother.

"Then can my friends come round here to play with me?" asked Andrew.

"Goodness, no!" cried his mother. "We don't want them to catch measles, too!"

So poor Andrew had to stay there all by himself. He felt very lonely. Then, one day, a hippo went past his window.

The hippo looked in. It gave a wink, and wiggled its ears. Then it went away again.

Andrew was very surprised. His bedroom was upstairs in the house, high above the ground. "That must be a very strange hippo," he thought. "He must have long legs!"

He asked his mother about the hippo. She hadn't seen it. She'd never heard of a hippo with long, long legs.

"I guess you were dreaming," she said. "You didn't *really* see a hippo."

"Yes, perhaps I dreamed it," said Andrew. "Whoever heard of a long-legged hippo?"

But the next day, the same hippo went past his window again!

Andrew waved and shouted to the hippo. It stopped and waggled its ears at him. Then it opened its great mouth and said something. It had a deep, mumbly voice, but Andrew couldn't hear what it was saying, because his window was closed.

The hippo went away again.

The next day was a very fine, sunshiny day.

Andrew asked his mother to leave his window wide open, and she did.

Andrew waited and waited, hoping that the strange hippo would come back.

Then, quite suddenly, there it was, with its big head sticking right in through the window.

"Hello, Andrew!" said the hippo. "How are you feeling today?"

"I'm feeling much better, thank you," said Andrew politely. Then he said, "You must be a very strange hippo, because you have such long legs."

"Not at all," said the hippo. "My legs are very ordinary hippo legs." It put its foot on Andrew's window ledge.

Andrew could see the hippo's whole leg. It *was* an ordinary, short, fat hippo leg.

"But what are you standing on?" cried Andrew. He was most surprised!

"Nothing at all!" laughed the hippo. "I don't need to stand on anything, because I have wings!"

Then it flitted up and down and around in front of the window, and showed off its wings. They were lovely wings – long and strong, and shiny!

Andrew thought the flying hippo was the most beautiful creature he'd ever seen! Soon they were very good friends. The hippo sang songs and told jokes, and kept Andrew company for hours.

It came back every day after that, and Andrew didn't feel lonely any more.

The best day was when Andrew was better, and his mother let him get out of bed. Then the hippo took him for a ride on its back. They flew over the town and home again.

Andrew climbed from the hippo's back, through his window, and into his room. "Will you give me another ride tomorrow?" he asked.

"No, Andrew, I'm sorry, but I won't be coming back again," said the friendly hippo. "You're better now, and you don't really need me to visit you any more. I must go and cheer up the other sick children who have to stay in bed."

Then the hippo waggled its ears, flipped its tail, and flew away. Andrew never saw it again, but he never forgot the friendly hippo.

The Little House

Susan badly wanted the dolls' house that stood in the window of the toy shop.

It was a beautiful house, with windows and doors that opened, a red roof, and two big chimneys.

So she started to save up her pocket money, but every time she counted it, there was nowhere near enough.

Then one day, as she was going home, she looked in the toy shop, and her dolls' house was gone.

She cried and cried all the way home. Later she went out to the park, but she did not feel like playing with the other children, so she sat under the trees and thought about her lovely dolls' house.

As she sat there, trying hard not to cry any more, she saw something moving among the flowers. At first she thought it was a bird, but as she sat very still and looked closely she saw that it was something dragging a large twig covered in leaves.

Then she saw it was a little man, no bigger than her hand when she stretched out her fingers wide, and he was dragging the twig towards her.

Of course she did not move. She hardly dared to breathe as the little man looked out from between the flowers; then when he was sure there was no one about he started to drag the twig towards one of the trees.

It took a long time, even though he stopped and pulled off several of the leaves to make it lighter.

At last he got it to the tree, and then Susan saw him go up to the tree and tap it.

As soon as he did, a tiny little door at the bottom opened and in he went. Very soon he was out again, carrying a tiny little axe, and with it he quickly chopped the twig into pieces.

Susan thought she must be dreaming, but she could hear the tap, tap, tap, just like a woodpecker, so she knew she was not.

As soon as he had finished, he carried the pieces into his house, one at a time. Susan could see how tired he was by the time he fetched in the last piece of wood and shut the door.

A few minutes later Susan saw a little puff of smoke coming out of a hole higher up the tree, and she knew that the little man had lit his fire and would be warming himself in his little home.

Then she remembered it was getting late, but before she left she picked up a few twigs and put them close to the front door of the little man's house.

The next evening she went back to the park and she saw that her twigs were gone. So she fetched some more and put them close to the door again, and as she did so she was certain she could see a little eye looking through a hole in the side of the tree, not very far from the door.

It was very cold that week, but each evening she went to the park by herself and put a few more twigs by the tiny door, and each time she found that the last bunch had been taken.

On Saturday she was later than usual, because she had been shopping with her mother, and when she got to her tree the door was open and the little man was shivering just inside.

So she hurried to get the twigs, and as she put them down he darted out and carried them in, one at a time, until he had as many as he could store.

Then he waved goodbye, shut the door, and very soon a puff of smoke appeared at the hole in the side of the tree.

After that, each evening Susan would find the little man waiting outside his house and as she put down the twigs he would carry them in, and wave goodbye when he had enough.

Susan had so much fun watching the little man that she soon forgot about the dolls' house. She hadn't forgotten about her dolls, though. They still needed a house, so she decided to make one for them.

And if you turn the page, you will see how to make a house for your dolls.

How to Make a Little Dolls' House

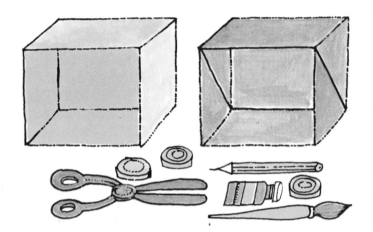

You will need: 2 cardboard boxes, pencil, scissors, paints or crayons

One of the boxes will be the house and one will be the roof. Look at the drawing on the right. This is the box that will be used for the roof of the house. It has been cut diagonally from one corner to another in order to make the roof-shape shown below it. Now look at the box you intend to use for the roof. Make sure that this diagonal line is *longer* than the width of the other box (the house) from front to back. (The back of the house is the open side.) Draw the two diagonal lines, cut along these lines, and along the base, as shown. With the pencil draw the windows and the door on the other box.

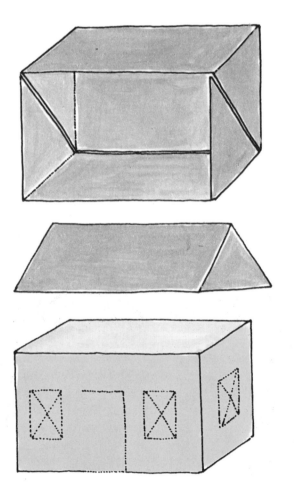

Starting from the center of each window, cut to each corner and then along the shape of the window until it is completely cut out. Cut the bottom, top, and one side of the door. Leave the other side as a hinge.

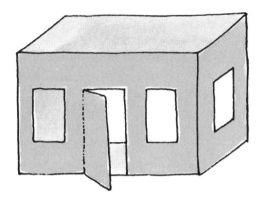

Put on the roof of the house, as shown. Decorate the house with paints or crayons. When the house is finished you can make furniture for it. Pieces of foam rubber can be used to make sofas and chairs. Bend pipe cleaners to make modern chair legs, lamps, etc. Cut a coffee-table shape from a matchbox, and a bed from a larger box. Make a bedspread and cover the foam furniture with scraps of cloth. Sinks and bathtubs can be carved from soap. If you use your imagination you will probably think of all sorts of things that can be made from various bits and pieces.

The Railroad

Stephen lived in a little house a long way from the village.

All around were fields and woods, and there was a big garden with trees and flowers, and at the end of the garden there was a tall, strong fence.

Stephen often used to climb onto the fence and look over it, for on the other side was a railroad track.

He loved to watch the trains go by, and would wave to the driver and passengers, and he always knew when a train was near.

The first train each day he would hear in bed, and then he would know it was time to get up.

Then another train would pass at midday, and a third at tea-time, and when the last train went by he knew it was time for bed.

One day his mother told him he must put all his toys into a box and pack up his books and clothes, because they were going away to live in the city.

At first he was very excited and was busy packing everything away, but he was a little sad when he sat on the fence and waved good-bye to his train for the last time.

Very soon Stephen arrived at his new home and all day was busy unpacking and putting his toys and books on their shelves, until, very tired, he went to bed.

The next morning his mother called him to breakfast.

"But the train has not gone past yet," he answered.

"You won't hear it today," said his mother. "It is a long way away now."

And then Stephen was very sad. He began to miss his train, and when he did not hear it at midday, or tea-time, and when there was no whistle at bedtime, he lay in bed and cried and cried until he fell asleep.

The next day he walked around the garden, which was small and had no trees, and wished and wished that he were back in his old home, with the railroad track.

Then he went down to the fence at the end of the garden to see what was there, and climbed up to look over.

There was a much bigger garden on the other side, with lawns and seats and trees and a pond with ducks swimming on it.

At the far end of the garden was a large house with huge chimneys and lovely big windows that opened out on to the lawn.

Stephen stood on a rail of the fence for a long time, looking at the garden and the big house, but wishing that he was really looking out at his railroad.

Then a little old man came out of the house and slowly walked down the garden, past the ducks on the pond, and across to where Stephen was watching.

"Hello," he said.

"Hello," said Stephen. "I was looking at your garden."

"Do you like gardens?" asked the man.

"Not very much," said Stephen. "I would rather look at trains. I used to listen to the trains every day, and watch them when I could, and now I miss them very much."

"I love trains, too," said the little old man. "I have been collecting pictures and models all my life. Would you like to see some?"

"Oh, yes, please," said Stephen.

"Then run and ask your mother, and I will show you."

Stephen ran back to the house, calling, "Mother, Mother, I want to see the trains."

"What is the matter with you?" said his mother. "You know there are no trains here."

He told her what the man had said, and

she came down the garden to see him. He told her his name was Mr. Adams, and while they were talking Stephen climbed over the fence.

When they got to the house, Mr. Adams led Stephen into a large room. He stopped and gasped.

All the way around the room were railroad tracks, with dozens of little engines and little cars standing on them. There was a beautiful station, with platforms and gardens and trees on one side, and signals and telephone lines beside the tracks, which ran through tunnels and over bridges.

After a long time Stephen heard Mr. Adams saying, "Would you like to see them moving?"

He nodded. Somehow he could not speak.

Then Mr. Adams led him across to a table in one corner of the room and told him to press a big button.

At once all the lights on the platforms lit up, and the trains started to move, some one way and some another.

Some moved very slowly, as though the cars were filled with heavy loads, and some moved very fast, like express trains going to the cities, and as they passed the signals the lights changed from green to red, and back again, just as they did on his railroad in the country.

Mr. Adams showed Stephen how to move the levers to stop the trains or make them go backwards. He showed him how to make them go from one track to another, and stop in the station, or go into their sheds.

After a long, long time Stephen realized it was past the time for his tea, and his mother would be worried, but he did not want to leave the wonderful railroad.

"You must come again," said the old man. "I do not come in here often now, but if you would like to join me sometimes it will be much more fun."

So whenever he could, which was very often, Stephen would climb over the fence and go to play with Mr. Adams' wonderful model trains.

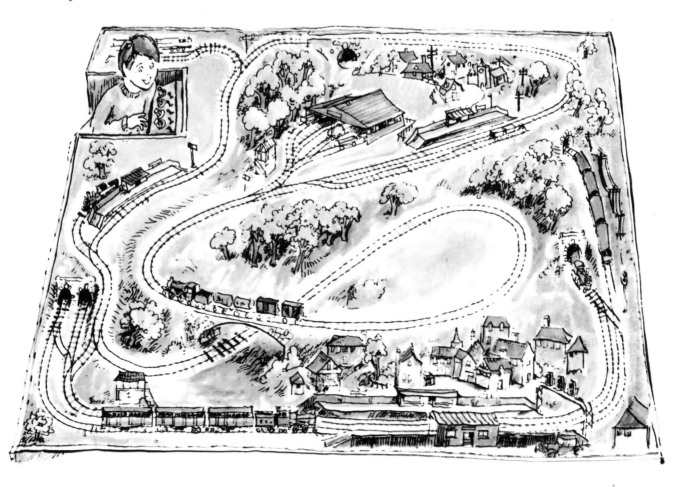

Paul's Book

Paul was ill. After a week in bed, he was bored. He had read all his books. He had played with all his games and toys.

One morning his mother showed him a letter.

"Your aunt in Canada has sent us a letter. She would like you to write to her."

"What shall I write?" asked Paul.

"Write about yourself," said his mother. "I will get some paper."

Paul began to write about himself. He wrote about his home and his school. Then he wrote about his holidays at the seaside. He told his aunt about his friends and his pets. After that, he drew pictures of all the things he had written about.

"You have written a book!" said his mother, smiling. "Your aunt will be very pleased."

Have you ever written a book about yourself?

The Tree House

In the far corner of Flockton Farm, a long way from the house, stands a huge beech tree. It is on the edge of a large green field, but the grass does not grow beneath its spreading branches; instead the earth is bare and hard with only a few of the beech tree's great roots showing above it.

The beech tree has a thick, greenish trunk and the lower branches, which are also very thick, grow out parallel to the ground. In the summer the leaves make it impossible to see into the heart of the tree.

Behind the tree the fields stretch peacefully to the farmhouse where Mr. Chambers lives. He and his sons farm the land growing corn, hops, potatoes, and beans. They have some cows and a large flock of chickens. Everyone in the district buys Mr. Chambers' eggs, which are large and brown.

In front of the tree, on the other side of the fence, the ground dips down to a clear stream. Beyond that are the gardens of the cottages where Stephen and Suzy live, next door to their friend Paul.

The beech tree has provided many different creatures with homes over the years.

For several years a family of squirrels had their nest high above the ground. The baby squirrels would scamper along the broad branches as easily as you or I might run along the ground.

Then there was the woodpecker who pecked out a home for herself with her hard beak. A pigeon laid her eggs in the same hole two years later.

For a while an owl spent his days in the shadiest part of the tree, where he had a regular perch, and of course there had been many sparrows, robins, thrushes and blackbirds building their nests among the maze of branches.

The three friends, Stephen, Suzy, and Paul, liked the enormous tree and had often played together beneath its shady branches, but they had never been able to climb it.

"I'm sure it would be very easy to climb, once we reached the first branches," said Paul one day.

Stephen had suggested taking down the swing in their apple tree and using the rope to climb the beech tree.

This seemed a good idea and a fine way to spend the morning, so they were soon back with two pieces of rope tied together, trying to throw it over a branch seven or eight feet above them. Paul managed it and tied a slip knot to make it secure enough for Stephen, the best climber, to scramble up onto the branch.

He then moved the rope nearer the trunk and the others were able to climb up with their feet against the tree trunk.

They were delighted when they had all climbed up, since it was so easy to clamber around the tree. Some branches were so broad and level that they could balance along them without holding on.

Suzy, who could climb nearly as well as the boys, wanted to make the rope into a rope ladder so that they could come along and play in the tree whenever they liked.

Stephen, Suzy, and Paul started visiting the tree almost every day, so the new rope ladder – which had taken a whole day to make – was left tied to a convenient branch. They claimed their own favorite perches where they would sit and talk to each other across the tree.

Paul noticed how level the branches in the middle were and said, "We could build a platform across them for sitting on."

"Even better," said Stephen, "let's try to build a real tree house."

The three friends were very excited and now spent the long summer days scrounging unwanted wood from the farm and taking it

to the tree on Stephen's wheelbarrow. The rubbish dump provided them with lots of old rope, wood, and, most exciting, an old pulley, which would be splendid for hauling the heavy planks into the tree.

"What on earth are you going to do with all that wood?" Mr. Chambers had asked, but they didn't want to tell him, as the beech tree was on his land. Instead they made vague replies about a secret den – which were almost true.

Now the really hard work began. The longest, strongest planks were hoisted up on the pulley which had been fitted with a strong, new rope.

The planks were laid across the most level

branches and were so secure that they only needed to be kept in place by rope tied around the ends of the planks and the branch they were on. This pleased everyone, as they wanted to avoid knocking nails into the tree.

It took two days to make the platform, which sloped up a little in one corner, and when it was finished they all sat together on it feeling extremely pleased with the progress.

"The walls and roof aren't going to be so easy," said Stephen, who had become the engineer because he always seemed to know the best way to do things.

After several unsuccessful ideas they found that two thick poles, tied to branches above the platform, formed a solid structure, and they all got busy nailing planks and scrap wood from these to the platform to make the walls.

"It looks a bit strange," giggled Suzy, "with Ceylon Tea on one side and Oranges from Florida on the other."

But everything was going well. All that was needed was a roof.

"We really need corrugated iron for that," said Stephen, "but there's none at the dump or anywhere else that I can think of."

"We haven't got enough wood to do the job, either," said Paul gloomily. "It ought to be waterproof, anyway."

"Waterproof? Waterproof?" mused Stephen. "I know!" he exclaimed, hopping wildly around the roofless tree house. "Our tent! I bet we could make a terrific roof if we fixed it right across the walls."

So the tent was brought quickly to the beech tree, and it fitted over the four walls beautifully.

The three friends scrambled inside when the corners had been secured and marveled at how much room there was. As if to test the new roof a shower of rain began to penetrate the leaves of the beech tree. As the rain drummed pleasantly on the canvas the three friends sat in the completed tree house and happily planned the days ahead.

It was decided that the tree house should be kept a secret. Stephen cleverly fixed up a rope, looped over a branch and tied to the ladder so they could hoist it out of sight when they left for home or were in their tree. They weren't quite sure whether the farmer would mind them using his tree. One day, when Mr. Chambers passed near the beech tree on his tractor, they all kept quiet, and of course the leaves hid them from sight.

What marvelous days they had, inventing all sorts of games to play around the tree house. A favorite was Swiss Family Robinson, which they had all read. They pretended that this was their stronghold and that they had to fight off savages and keep a lookout for ships on the horizon.

On sunny days they discovered that it was fun to open the flaps of the tent to make a sort of sunshine roof. When there was a shower, however, they all sat inside the tree house and closed the door, which was an old sack hung over the hole.

They brought two orange boxes to use as cupboards for their own special treasures: tin mugs, water bottles, wooden swords for playing pirates, Stephen's six-gun, Paul's old knife with all its gadgets, and Suzy even had a pair of tiny binoculars which she used to look out for imaginary but wicked enemies.

Often they spent the whole day in the tree, drawing the rope ladder up after them and playing or reading adventure stories and eating sandwiches at lunch time.

The summer vacation was drawing to a close and the tree home was still a secret.

"I wish we could spend a whole vacation in the tree," said Suzy, "and not have to go home at all."

"We could spend a night here," said Paul.

"No, we wouldn't be allowed to do that."

"Then it will have to be a secret, our last big adventure in the tree house before going back to school," was Stephen's excited reply.

All that week they made plans.

"We mustn't stay all night. We have to be back in our beds before morning," said Suzy sensibly.

"I suppose so, but it will still be fun to come in the dark with a feast and a book of ghost stories to read aloud," laughed Stephen.

So at eleven o'clock on Friday night they climbed out their bedroom windows and met under the full moon at the end of Paul's garden. They had on warm sweaters and carried sacks with their feast inside, a flashlight, and a book of ghost stories. They set off for the tree house feeling very adventurous.

Paul got a wet foot as he was crossing the stream and they giggled a little as they climbed up the bank and under the fence to the tree.

It was darker beneath the canopy of leaves, so when they pulled the rope ladder down, Stephen held the flashlight while Suzy and Paul climbed up. Then Paul lit a candle in a jam jar which had been left in the tree house and held that for Stephen to see by as he followed them up the swaying rope ladder.

Once inside the familiar tree house it was really marvelous. The candle lit the red wigwam roof and set their shadows flickering round the walls.

The leaves rustled outside and an owl hooted mournfully, which made them jump in spite of themselves.

"It's exciting," they reassured each other. "Let's have our feast right away."

Out came the sandwiches, potato chips, and chocolate, and they passed around a huge bottle of lemonade, laughing about the adventure they were having.

Stephen insisted on reading a ghost story, but the others didn't like the idea much. The book was called *Eight Strange Stories*. Stephen started to read one called "The Legend of Sleepy Hollow." They were all beginning to feel rather tense as the story became frightening. Then suddenly Stephen stopped reading and sat quietly with his head on one side.

"I'm sure I heard a noise," he whispered, making a sign to keep quiet.

They all listened. There *were* noises—

rustlings and a cracking of twigs as if someone were approaching the tree.

Suzy was terrified and wished she had stayed at home.

"Come on," said a deep voice from below. "We haven't got all night."

"Wait here a minute," said another voice, "and make sure it's all clear."

"Let's check all the gear. Have you got the skeleton keys?"

" 'Course I have, and the sacks and flashlight. For heaven's sake be ready to run at the first sign of trouble."

They talked a little longer and then moved off to the left of the tree. They had said enough for all the wide-eyed adventurers in the tree to know that they intended to steal Mr. Chambers' chickens.

"What do you think we should do?" Paul whispered.

"Mr. Whiteman over at Valley Farm had sixty chickens stolen last week," said Stephen. "There's only one thing we can do now – warn Mr. Chambers."

They all climbed down the rope ladder as quietly as possible, crouching on the ground and trying to see the men, but they had moved out of sight.

"We'll cut across to the next field on the right and up to the trees," decided Stephen.

Off they filed, keeping crouched down at first. Then, once they had the protection of a thick hedge, they straightened up and ran as fast as they could for the trees.

The dew on the long grass soaked their legs and feet, and their breathing became heavy as they panted up the slope. But the full moon provided plenty of light to see the way. On reaching the edge of the trees Stephen and Paul waited, panting, for Suzy, who had lagged behind.

It was dark in the wood but luckily Suzy knew all the paths, since she used to come exploring with one of her friends. She led the way to the other side and they emerged in just the right spot for a last dash to the farmhouse.

As they clattered into the farm yard, two Labrador dogs began to bark and rattle their chains, making a terrific noise.

Upstairs a window flew open and Mr. Chambers demanded, "Who's that down there?"

Stephen could hardly get his breath but managed to gasp out, "Two men are stealing your chickens."

"Wait there," Mr. Chambers called.

Lights went on in the farmhouse and soon the farmer and his two strapping sons ran out the back door, asking the children how they knew and where they had seen the men.

They quickly told them as much as they knew.

By now Mr. Chambers was at the wheel of his car, and his sons had jumped into the back.

"You go back into the house," he shouted as the car roared off down the drive, headlights blazing.

They went in the back door. Mrs. Chambers, looking rather worried, was standing in her dressing gown. She wanted to know exactly what was happening as she shepherded them into the warm kitchen and began preparing some cocoa.

The secret of the tree house had to be broken, so they told her all about building it and the events that led up to hearing the men plan the robbery.

"Heavens, your parents will be worried sick, you naughty children!" exclaimed Mrs. Chambers. "I must 'phone them right away and tell them you are all safe."

When she left them sipping cocoa, they looked guiltily at each other but didn't say anything, each wondering if there would be trouble about the tree house and the night's escapade.

Before long, however, Mr. Chambers came bursting in, followed by his sons, looking very pleased.

"Caught them red-handed!" He beamed. "We picked up a policeman on the way and just got to the chicken houses as they were breaking in. They had keys and everything."

"That should put an end to the chicken stealing in this area," said Mrs. Chambers.

They all sat round the kitchen drinking cocoa and pieced together the story from the beginning.

Mr. Chambers didn't mind a bit about the tree house. In fact he was highly amused that they had kept it so secret. He couldn't get over the coincidence of the friends choosing the same night as the thieves for their adventure.

"You got more of an adventure than you bargained for," he laughed.

He assured them that he would explain everything to their parents, for he was very pleased with their night's work.

"I'm only going to the tree house during the day from now on," said Suzy, and the boys joined in the laughter – not wanting to admit that they, too, had been frightened.

around the world

You will need: a colored counter for each person, two spinners (p. 156). This game is for any number of players.

If you wish you can make the small boats shown below and use these instead of counters. Start by putting your boat on the red square in the middle of the board. First spin the direction spinner: this tells you whether to go north, south, east, or west. Then spin the number spinner: this tells you how many squares to move in that direction. The winner is the player who goes off the edge of the board first. You must spin the exact number and direction to finish.

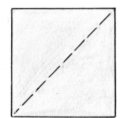
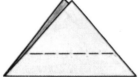

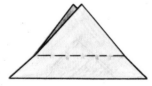

To make the boats for this game, cut a square out of stiff paper the same size as ours above. Fold it in half from corner to corner. Fold up the bottom edge a little way and stick it into a piece of clay.

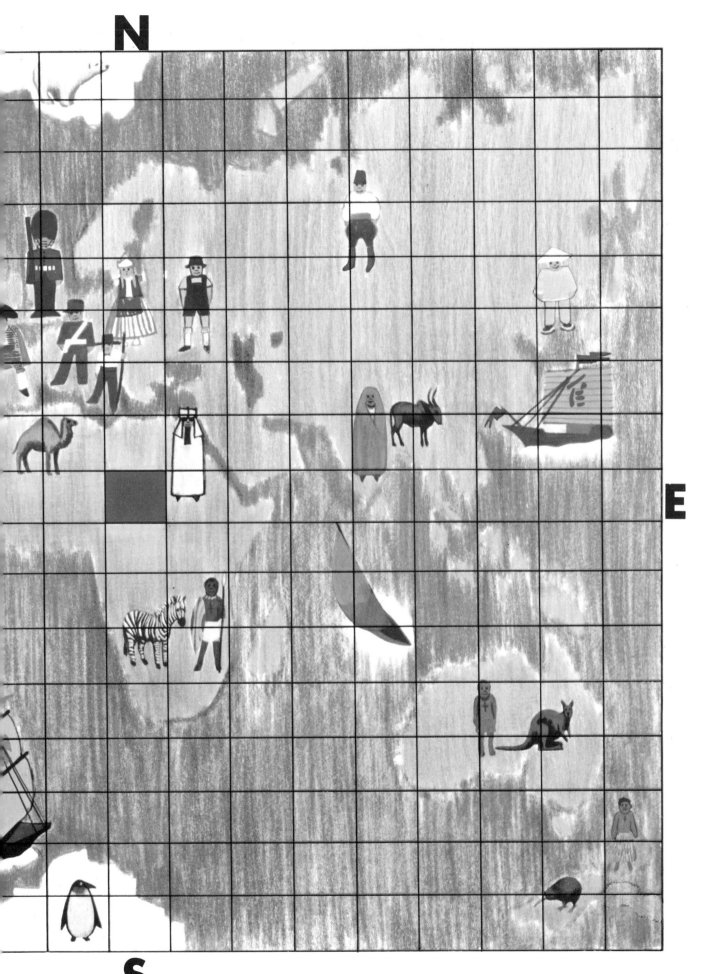

N

S

E

61

Blackie's Walk

Blackie was a dog. He lived in a big town. He went for walks in the park, away from the cars. But sometimes it was shut, so Blackie stayed in his garden.

A cat lived next door. Blackie did not like her. But he liked the birds. They talked to him. A bird sitting in a tree said, "I have been flying for a long time."

"Where have you been?" asked Blackie.

"I have been outside the town," said the bird. "I have been over farms and fields."

"Are there any cars there?" asked Blackie.

"No, not many," said the bird.

"I wish I could go there," said Blackie. "Then I could run around as much as I like."

"I can take you," said the bird. "I will show you the way. I will fly there and you can watch me and come behind."

Blackie watched the bird and ran behind it down the road. But soon he could not see it. It had gone right up into the sky. Blackie stopped. He was on a road which he did not know. Which way had the bird gone?

Blackie ran around, looking. All he could see
were cars and buses. He did not know which
way to go. The bird did not come back.

Then he found that he had come a very long
way. He could not find his home. He walked
around and around.

Then all at once Blackie saw the cat who
lived next door. He forgot he did not like the
cat. He ran up to her.

"How can I get back to my garden?" he asked.

The cat was glad that Blackie had talked to

her. She often saw Blackie over the fence.

"I will take you," she said. "I know the way.
I often go out walking."

Blackie walked down the road after the cat.
Soon he could see his own house.

"It is better to go with you than with the
bird," said Blackie.

"If you like," said the cat, "I'll show you some
good places to go."

"Oh, thank you," said Blackie. "We will go
for walks together every day."

Edgar and Egbert Cross the River

Come on, Egbert. Let's eat those lovely berries.

Brrrr! The water's too cold!
I know! I'll cross by the stepping stones so my feet won't get wet!

Don't do that!!!
Why not, Edgar?
Because the water's very deep there.

Is it?

OOOOOO ! ! ! ! I'm slipping . . . .

SPLASH!
Yeeee ! ! !

Haw haw haw! I told you so, Egbert!
I don't think it was funny!

But *that* is! Enjoy your slide, Edgar ?
Yow!

words

kite

balloons

lighthouse

boat

flowers

toy duck

cc

dog

snail

bird

statue

flag

airplane

clock

windmill

sea

ladder

brush

bucket

Indoor Gardens

Morning–glories

You will need: flower pot (about 5 inches across the top), morning-glory seeds, soil or potting compost, liquid fertilizer
May is the best time to plant morning-glories. Before planting, soak them in water for a day. Plant five seeds, about 1 inch deep, in the pot. Water the soil or compost after planting. Set the pot in a dark, warm place. In 2-4 days, at the first sign of sprouting, put the pot in a dimly lit place. Next day move it into full light. At first, keep the compost damp, by giving it a little water every few days. As morning-glories grow, they'll need more watering. When they're in bloom, they need a big drink every day and liquid fertilizer every 3-4 days. In very hot weather, water twice a day. When the plants are about two weeks old, take out the smallest ones, leaving three plants in the pot. Tie three strings around the rim of the pot and fasten the other ends of the strings at the top of the window. The plants will merrily clamber up, and burst into beautiful blue trumpets about six weeks after planting.

Blotting Paper Garden

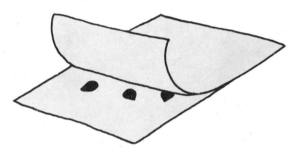

You will need: blotting paper, seeds
There are many kinds of seeds that will grow between two layers of damp blotting paper. Seeds from most fruits can be grown in this way. Try it with apple seeds or orange pips. Keep the paper moist. After three or four weeks the seeds should begin to sprout. Put them in earth in a pot.

Flower Pot Holders

You will need: round plastic tubs (soft margarine is sold in them), crayons
Wash and dry the tubs. Draw designs on the outsides with crayons.

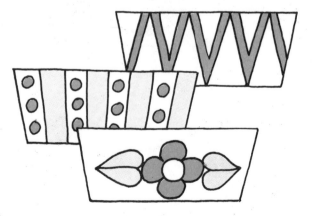

Stowaway

It was blissfully warm on board the S.S. *Penrose*, a passenger liner on its way to the South. Jane was traveling with her parents. In the afternoon she liked to sit in the cool shade of a lifeboat. Down below, the waves were rushing past. Watching them made her sleepy.

"Meow."

Jane sat up, rubbing her eyes. It sounded like a cat.

"Meow."

There it was again. It seemed to come from the lifeboat above. Jane climbed up to the lifeboat and saw that a corner of the tarpaulin was loose. Looking inside she saw a lovely ginger-colored cat. Jane played with the cat all afternoon, and gave it a name: Marmalade.

That evening Jane surprised her mother very much because she asked for fish as the first course and fish as the main course.

"But you never eat fish," said her father. Jane said that she had suddenly developed a craving for it. Then she began to nibble her fish – ugh!, she still did not like it, but hoped it did not show, as her parents were watching. Dinner over, Jane managed to slide a large piece of fish into her napkin, slipping it all into her little bag.

"You ate that fish quickly," said her mother.

"It made me thirsty," answered Jane. "Can I have a glass of milk and take it out on deck, Mummy?"

"Yes, of course, darling," said her mother.

Jane rushed out to the lifeboat, where Marmalade was hiding. He drank the milk so fast that she had to hold on to the glass. Then he ate all the fish and soon rolled over and fell asleep. Jane tiptoed to her cabin and felt very happy.

After a few days Jane's mother began to worry because all that Jane would eat was fish – and lots of it! And yet, Jane did not look well, rather thin, and she disappeared every evening. So, one evening, Jane's mother decided to follow her on deck. She saw Jane climb into one of the lifeboats and she quietly walked over to it. What a surprise she had when she looked inside and found Jane feeding milk and fish to a ginger-colored cat. She said: "What a lovely cat you have here—but why didn't you tell me about it?"

"I wanted to keep it a secret, Mummy, because cats are not allowed on board. I have been feeding it every day; its name is Marmalade."

"How kind of you, my dear," said Jane's mother, thinking of all the fish Jane so obviously had not eaten. "I will see what I can do to help you and Marmalade."

The captain was on the bridge deck.

"A passenger to see you, sir," announced the Captain's Steward. It was Jane's father, and he told the captain about Jane, the cat, and the fish. "Is there anything you could do?" he asked.

"So that's what it is all about!" smiled the captain. "I often saw your little girl walk across the deck with a glass of milk in her

hand. Of course, we have our rules, sir; no animals on deck. But I believe I have found an answer: I shall keep the cat up here on the bridge as a mascot!"

The same day a little box was made by the ship's carpenter, a box for Marmalade to sleep in. Every evening Jane was allowed to come right up to the bridge to feed Marmalade. She could, at last, eat her chicken and steaks again and soon looked much better. After dinner every evening the steward brought Jane some fish wrapped in a napkin and a glass of milk. He smiled and said: "For our mascot."

Little Bear – The Indian Boy

High in the Great Smoky Mountains, Little Bear, the Indian boy, sat on his horse, listening. He knew all the sounds of the forest, and he knew that an animal was following him. It could have been a timber wolf or a wild boar, but Little Bear did not think so. He was a good tracker, and when he saw a flame azalea blossom on the ground, or a broken twig, he could read these signs like a book. That morning he had seen the tracks of a young bear, and as he waited he caught sight of a black mountain bear among the yellow poplar trees. Little Bear knew how to defend himself and he was not afraid. He could shoot a bow and arrow, and in his belt he had a hunting knife and a hatchet. After this the Indian boy often saw the bear. He liked wild honey, and sometimes when he traced the honeybees to a hollow tree the bear would follow. It liked honey, too.

Little Bear was a Cherokee Indian and his tribe lived near the Oconaluftee River. One day he thought he would go exploring on the river, so he paddled off downstream in his dugout canoe which had been hollowed out of a big log. When the sun was high in the sky, he tied up the canoe and found a clear space where he made a fire by rubbing a flint on a stone. His mother had given him corn meal cakes and deer meat to roast so he only had to pick some berries and drink some ice-cold water from the stream which came rushing down the mountain side. As he began to eat he heard leaves rustling and there stood the black bear.

Little Bear was sorry he could not speak to the bear in its own language. The old men of his tribe said that once upon a time all living things spoke the same language, but men behaved badly and the Great One who lived in the sky punished them. He made them deaf to the language of the animals and birds, and now men could only understand each other.

"Sta-yee-ju," said Little Bear in Cherokee language. This means, "Are you well?" and is just like saying, "How are you?" He didn't close his lips at all when he spoke because you can pronounce all the sounds in the Cherokee language, except one, without closing your lips. The bear grunted and came closer. Little Bear gave it some of his food.

Sitting cross-legged by the fire in his deerskin trousers with his necklace of bear's teeth, he said to the bear: "When I am a man I shall be a great chief like my father. I shall do brave deeds and pass many tests and then I will get an eagle feather and I will wear it all my life to show that I am a warrior."

The bear grunted again.

"Now I must go," said Little Bear, but suddenly a rattlesnake darted out and he had to jump clear. His foot slipped on a loose stone and he twisted his ankle. He couldn't walk. The bear stayed by his side and licked him.

"How long will it be before they find me?" thought Little Bear. "I may have to stay here all night, and a wolf may find me first." Then he saw that the bear had gone away.

At the Cherokee village Little Bear's big brother, Running Wolf, was chipping flints into arrowheads when he noticed a bear on the other side of the river. Picking up his bow and arrow he jumped into his canoe, but the bear lumbered away. He could hear it crashing through the trees. He thought he had lost it but the bear kept appearing

as if it wanted to make sure that Running Wolf was following. At last the bear came out into the open.

"Now," thought Running Wolf, "I shall get myself a fine bearskin." He raised his bow, ready to shoot. He could not miss. Suddenly he heard a loud cry – "No! No!" It was his brother, Little Bear. Throwing down his bow, Running Wolf leaped out of the canoe and ran to his little brother.

"You nearly shot my friend," said Little Bear, and although he was a very manly little Indian boy there were tears in his eyes. Then he smiled. Everything would be all right now.

Sing a song of sixpence,
A pocket full of rye;
Four-and-twenty blackbirds
Baked in a pie.
When the pie was opened,
The birds began to sing;
Wasn't that a dainty dish
To set before the king?

Little Jack Horner
Sat in the corner,
Eating his Christmas pie;
He put in his thumb
And pulled out a plum,
And said, "What a good boy am I!"

Mary had a little lamb,
Its fleece was white as snow;
And everywhere that Mary went,
The lamb was sure to go.

Little Miss Muffet sat on a tuffet,
Eating her curds and whey;
Along came a spider who sat down beside her
And frightened Miss Muffet away.

Humpty Dumpty sat on a wall,
Humpty Dumpty had a great fall;
All the king's horses and all the king's men
Couldn't put Humpty together again.

Nursery Rhyme Puzzle

Can you match up the nursery rhymes
on the left with the mixed-up pictures
below?

All Change
for the Holidays!

Mr. and Mrs. Paul Pudding and their seven
dumpling children lived in a big house, high
on a mountain.

One summer day Mrs. Pudding said to
Mr. Pudding, "I feel like a change. I'd like
to go to the seaside for a holiday."

"But this is a lovely place for a holiday,
right here!" cried Mr. Pudding, who didn't
like making changes. "Lots of people come
to the mountains for a holiday."

"I know," said Mrs. Pudding, "but that's
not the same thing. I'd like a change. I'd
like to go to the seaside."

Mr. Pudding was going to say "No!" but
the little dumpling Puddings had heard
their mother say "seaside".

"Yes, yes! Let's go to the seaside," they
all cried.

Then Mr. Pudding had to say "Yes!" for
he knew he'd get no peace till he did.

So off they went, with fat Mr. and Mrs.
Pudding filling up the front seat of their
little car. The back was full of the seven
little dumpling Puddings.

They were halfway to the seaside when
the car broke down. Mr. Pudding sighed. He
hated fixing the car.

"I *told* you we shouldn't have come," he
said to Mrs. Pudding.

But she just laughed, and started talking
to some other people. Their car had broken
down, too. They were Mr. and Mrs. Gilbert
Thynne and their seven skinny little children, who were on their way to a holiday in
the mountains.

Mr. Thynne was sighing and complaining
as he repaired his car. "I don't know what
we'll do when we get there," he said. "I
said we shouldn't go to the mountains, for
when we get there we'll have no place to
stay."

"Why, you can use our house while we're
away," said Mrs. Pudding. "We're going to
the seaside for our holiday."

Mr. Thynne stopped sighing, and smiled
most happily. "Thank you," he said. "We'll
be glad to stay in your house. And while
you're at the seaside, you can stay in *our*
house. It's right by the beach!"

"Hooray!" shouted all the dumpling
Pudding children and all the skinny Thynne
children. Mr. Pudding and Mr. Thynne

traded the keys of their houses. Then they finished fixing their cars, and they all drove off to their holidays.

The Puddings thought the Thynnes' little house was just lovely. They had a bit of trouble because all the chairs and beds and tables were rather small for them, but they didn't mind.

Once, Mrs. Pudding got stuck in Mrs. Thynne's little armchair. It took Mr. Pudding and all the dumpling Puddings to pull her out of it again! But she didn't care. She thought it was a great joke!

They had a grand holiday. They all bobbed about in the sea, and played in the sand. There was a fairground, too, and they went to visit that.

One day they hired a little boat to go fishing. Big Mr. and Mrs. Pudding and all the little dumpling Puddings climbed aboard. But the water began running in over the sides. They were too heavy! So they all hopped out again. Then they found a good big boat, which didn't sink under them. They sailed out to sea and fished.

Mr. Pudding caught a huge fish. All the dumpling Pudding children caught little ones. They took the fish home and Mrs. Pudding cooked them. Then all the Puddings ate up all the fish.

When it was time to go home, the Pudding family felt sorry to leave the seaside. But they also thought it would be fine to go home again. So off they went.

Halfway home, they met the Thynnes, who were also halfway home. "We had a great holiday in the mountains, and we liked your house," said Mr. Thynne. "Once we lost Mrs. Thynne, because she'd fallen into Mrs. Pudding's big armchair. But we pulled her out, and she thought it was a good joke."

Everyone laughed at that. They said goodbye, and agreed to change houses for their holidays again.

So they did, and every year after that they all had wonderful holidays.

This Old Man

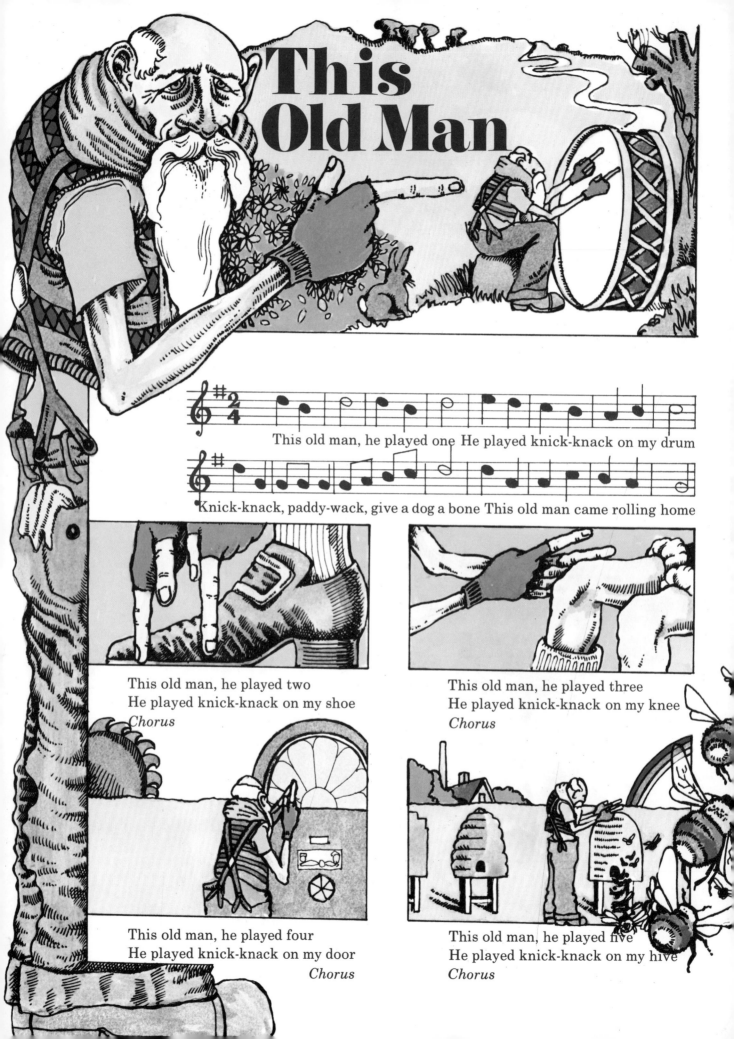

This old man, he played one He played knick-knack on my drum

Knick-knack, paddy-wack, give a dog a bone This old man came rolling home

This old man, he played two
He played knick-knack on my shoe
Chorus

This old man, he played three
He played knick-knack on my knee
Chorus

This old man, he played four
He played knick-knack on my door
Chorus

This old man, he played five
He played knick-knack on my hive
Chorus

This old man,
he played six
He played
knick-knack
on my sticks
Chorus

This old man, he played seven
He played knick-knack up in heaven *Chorus*

This old man, he played eight
He played knick-knack on my gate
Chorus

This old man, he played nine
He played knick-knack on my line
Chorus

This old man, he played ten
He played knick-knack on my hen

Chorus

Jamie's Sticks

Jamie was sitting in the kitchen of his old grandmother's cottage. The afternoon was getting colder, and their fire was burning low. His grandmother looked up from her doze.

"Jamie, be a good boy and fetch some logs for the fire, or we shall freeze tonight."

Jamie pulled on his coat and went out to the woodpile. He came back and said, "Granny, there are only these two little sticks left. The woodpile has been used up."

"Then go into the wood, Jamie, and pick up some sticks, or we shall freeze tonight."

Jamie put on his tattered cap and set off across the muddy fields, to the wood on the hill. He was a little afraid of the wood; it was full of strange sounds and movements, and he always felt that he was being watched. But they needed firewood, so he made up his mind to work quickly and leave as soon as possible.

He was not far into the trees when he spied a pile of sticks already in a heap. He hurried towards them, but just as he was stretching out his hand to pick them up a voice said, "Don't touch those, if you please."

Startled, Jamie swung round. Under a pair of long brown ears, a pair of round brown eyes were staring up at him from the bushes. It was a rabbit.

"I'm sorry," stammered Jamie. "I didn't know they belonged to anybody."

"Well, they do," replied the rabbit firmly. "Can't you read? That pile says in stick language 'Have gone out. Back in ten minutes.'"

"It's a message I left for the hedgehog," the rabbit continued. "He's coming to tea and I must go out and get in some goodies. If you want sticks, go a bit further into the

wood. Goodbye!" And off he ran, stirring up the dead leaves.

Jamie walked on, wondering about stick language. He was so occupied with his thoughts that he almost tripped over another heap of twigs.

"Well," he said aloud, "shall I take these, or are they another rabbit sign?"

"Rabbit sign!" came an indignant voice. "This is my house, and I'll thank you not to pull out my roof."

A tiny figure, dressed in green, was peering out from a hole in the twigs, presumably where the house window was.

"I'm sorry," apologized Jamie. "I'm just looking for wood. I've never seen an elf house before. I didn't realize . . ."

"I've already collected all the timber from hereabouts to build this house," said the elf. "If you want sticks, you'll have to go further on into the wood."

The forest was growing thicker now. Jamie's sharp eyes spotted a pile of small branches half-hidden behind an oak.

"Well," he said aloud, "I must take care. Is this a rabbit sign, or is it an elf house?"

"Don't be silly," came the reply. "Anyone can see that it's just a pile of sticks."

At last! thought Jamie, and stooped down to pick them up.

"Hey, what do you think you're doing?" shouted the voice crossly, and a small elf, dressed as a woodcutter, ran out from a clump of bushes, flourishing his axe.

"I'm taking this kindling home for the fire," explained Jamie.

"I collected those sticks!" cried the woodcutter elf. "You're not having the benefit of my labor. I've been ordered to fetch some wood to make a new bed for the king. Some misguided mole tunneled up under his old bed and broke it. So leave my wood alone, please."

"I'm sorry," said Jamie. "I didn't realize. But where can I find sticks, then?"

"Never mind, no harm done," replied the woodcutter elf, calming down. "I'm sorry I was so cross. But we're all rather on edge at the moment. The rooks have told us that our enemies, the trolls, are planning a big attack on us. They want to drive us out of our part of the wood and have it all to themselves. And I'm afraid that the only place you'll find any spare wood is in their territory, across the stream. We use all ours. Waste not, want not, we say."

"Trolls!" Jamie shivered. "But I must get some kindling from somewhere."

"You be very careful, then," warned the woodcutter. "We'd help you if we could, but the trolls have nasty sharp spears. Good luck!"

The woodcutter elf watched anxiously as Jamie waded across the stream. He climbed cautiously up the bank on the other side. He stopped suddenly as he heard voices, and made himself as invisible as possible behind a tree.

"This time we'll really get rid of those elves," chuckled a sinister voice.

"Yes, we've made enough spears now," came the answer. "It's taken us a long time, but it's worth it to be able to control the whole wood."

Jamie peeped warily round the tree. There, in a clearing, crouched two ugly trolls. Each had a stick in his hand, which he was sharpening to a nasty point.

"These two are the last two spears, then," said one. "If yours is ready, we'll take them along to the armory."

Jamie had an idea. If he followed the trolls and found their armory, he could seize all their spears. Then he'd be getting the spears as wood for the fire, and helping the elves at the same time. He crept along behind the two trolls and watched as they added their two spears to the huge heap that already filled a hollow tree. As soon as they had gone, Jamie seized his chance. He plunged his hands deep down into the hollow tree and scooped up an enormous armful of the weapons. They were much heavier than he had imagined. He staggered along through the trees, heading for the stream. Then he was spotted.

"A spy! A thief! After him!"

Trolls dashed out from all sides. Jamie ran

as fast as he could, panting, his arms straining under the weight of the spears and his heart thumping with fright. The first of the trolls reached the stream just as Jamie was halfway across. Shrieking at him, they lined the bank as Jamie flopped down on the other side and dropped his burden.

Hearing the commotion, the elves ran to him.

"The spears! You've captured the trolls' spears! We're saved!" they shouted with joy.

Jamie got his breath back. "I'm glad I got the right sticks at last," he said. "But now I must take them home to Grandmother for the fire."

"Leave that to us," said the elves. "That's the least we can do to thank you."

Grinning triumphantly at the trolls, who were beginning to disappear gloomily back into their own territory, each elf picked up a troll-spear. In a long, singing procession, the elves escorted Jamie all the way to his cottage, and dropped their spears down on his woodpile.

"Just one favor, if you please, before we go," asked the woodcutter elf. "May I have four of these spears?"

"Of course," answered Jamie. "I won't miss four from such a big pile. Why do you want them?"

The woodcutter elf wouldn't say. But that night, as he was going to bed after an evening around a lovely warm fire, Jamie guessed that the elf king would probably be having four troll-spears as bedposts.

Simple Printing

Potato Cut Prints

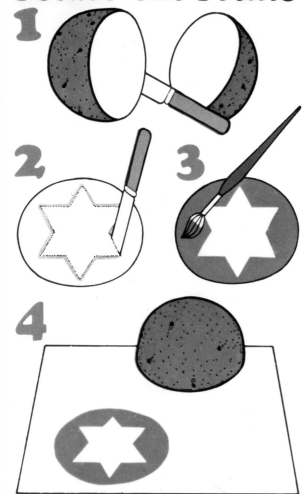

You will need: potato, knife, pencil, poster paints, paper

1. Wash and dry a potato and then cut it in half carefully with a knife.
2. Draw a simple shape on the cut surface and cut along the lines. Then scoop out the potato from the middle of the drawing.
3. Mix up some thick paint and cover the smooth surface. Do not paint the cut-out middle.
4. Now press the potato down onto clean paper. You will have printed your pattern.
5. Try printing some other patterns like ours. You can print shapes like the heart by cutting away the potato outside your drawing and leaving the middle. Try making a picture from your shapes.

Money Patterns

You will need: coins, thin paper, colored pencils

Put a coin under the paper and, holding it steady, rub all over with the pencil. Try this on other rough things like wood-grain and tree bark.

Clay Prints

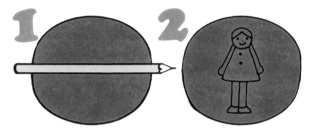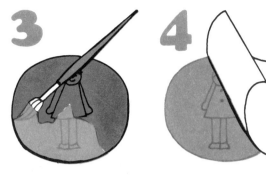

You will need: modeling clay, pencil, talcum powder, paint

1. Roll a piece of modeling clay out flat.
2. Draw a picture into it with the pencil.
3. Dust over the clay with talcum powder and then paint all over the clay.
4. Put a piece of paper over the clay and gently rub all over.
5. On the finished print the lines you have drawn will appear white on the color.

Making Stencils

You will need: paper, scissors, paint

1. Fold a square piece of paper in half and then in half again.
2. Cut off the corners of the square.
3. Open up the paper and see your stencil.
4. Put thick paint on another piece of paper larger than the stencil.

5. Now put the stencil on a piece of paper and the painted paper on top of that, paint-side down. Rub all over with your fingers.
6. The paint will print through the holes in the stencil.
7. Try printing through doilies. You can cut other shapes by drawing half the shape on a folded piece of paper and opening it up.

Rumpelstiltskin

Once, long ago, there lived a miller who had a very beautiful daughter. He was very proud of her, and thought nobody in all the land was fit to be her husband except the king himself.

Now one day, the king happened to ride past the miller's house while out hunting. The moment he saw the king, the miller rushed out and fell on his knees.

"Your Majesty," he said, "I have a daughter who is beautiful, good, kind, and clever."

"My good miller," replied the king, "the country seems to be full of fathers with beautiful, good, kind, and clever daughters for me to marry. What is so special about yours?"

The miller thought fast.

"Special? Well now, er ... *yes*! My daughter can spin straw into the purest gold. Now, I'm only a miller, but I call that very special indeed!"

"Why, yes, that *is* special," said the king. And he ordered the miller to send his daughter to the royal castle the next day.

Now the miller didn't dare tell his daughter of the story he had invented about her spinning gold from straw. "She's so beautiful," he thought, "the king will forget all about the gold when he sees her."

But the miller was wrong!

For when the girl was brought before the king, all he said was:

"Now, I've got a nice quiet little room waiting for you upstairs, with a nice pile of straw in it. Spin it into gold for me and I might start thinking of marrying you. Fail, and I'll chop off your head. And your father's, too!"

Then the king led her upstairs to a small room with nothing in it but a three-legged stool, a spinning wheel, and a big pile of straw.

"Goodnight, my dear," said the king. And then he left, locking the door behind him.

The moment she was alone the poor girl burst into tears. She cried and cried. But then, suddenly, she heard the door being unlocked. And in walked a tiny little man — so small that he came up only to her knee.

"What's this?" he said. "Crying? Dear me, we can't have that. What's the matter?"

When she told him, he laughed and said, "I can spin this straw into gold for you, but what will you give me for doing it?"

"I'll give you my necklace," the girl answered.

The little man nodded, sat down, and

began to spin. And while he worked he sang to himself:

> "Turn and spin
> Bright and bold,
> Turn the straw
> Into gold!"

When he had finished he got up and left, locking the door behind him.

In the morning when the king walked in, his eyes bulged. For in place of the pile of straw was a great hank of pure gold thread.

He was delighted. But not a word did he say about marrying the miller's daughter. In fact, he didn't say another word to her all day, but went off hunting instead. Then, that night, he took her by the arm and led her to a large room with nothing in it but a three-legged stool, a spinning wheel, and a great deal of straw.

"Just spin this straw into gold for me," the king said, "and then we'll discuss marriage. But do the spinning first."

And with that he turned and left, locking the door behind him.

Once again the miller's daughter sat down and started to cry. Once again she heard the door being unlocked, and once again, in came the funny little man.

"Ah, more straw to spin, I see," he said. "What will you give me to do it this time?"

"The ring from my finger," said the miller's daughter.

Then the little man nodded, sat down, and began to spin, singing to himself:

> "Turn and spin
> Bright and bold,
> Turn the straw
> Into gold!"

Next morning, the king was overjoyed—but still not satisfied.

And so, that night, he led the miller's daughter to his largest barn, and locked her in. Inside, the straw was piled from floor to rafters, and from end to end.

And so, for the third time the poor girl sat down and cried, and for the third time the funny little man unlocked the door and came in. The only difference was that this time she had nothing left to give him for spinning the gold for her.

"I know," said the little man, with a cunning look on his face. "I'll do it for a promise: just promise to give me the first

baby you have if you become queen."

Now, by this time, the miller's daughter didn't really think the king would ever marry her. All she wanted was to get safely out of the castle and back home. So she agreed to the little man's suggestion. Whereupon he sat down and began to spin, singing his little song. Quickly he spun all the straw into bright, shiny gold thread.

Now, the next morning, when the king came to the barn, he was so delighted at all the gold he found that he married the miller's daughter on the spot.

After that, for some time the king and his young queen lived very happily. He was so rich he didn't need to ask the queen to spin him any more gold, and she was so happy she forgot all about the funny little man.

But then the queen had a baby son, and one day, when he was just a few weeks old, and she was sitting all alone in her room playing with him, the door burst open and in marched the little man.

"Good morning, Your Majesty," he said. "Remember me? I've come for your child – you promised him to me and I want him."

The poor queen offered the little man all her money and jewels instead. But he wouldn't change his mind.

Then a wicked grin came over his face. "All the same, though," he said, "I think I'll give you a chance. If you can guess my name, I won't take your son. You can have three days to try, and three guesses each day. But if you don't guess it in that time, then I'll take your baby.

All that night the queen lay awake trying to guess the little man's name. Next day he came back.

"Is it Jeremiah?" she asked.

"No!" said the little man.

"Is it Ichabod?"

"No!"

"Then perhaps it is Cedrick?"

"Wrong again! You really must do better than this, you know – why, you've only got six chances left! Oh well, see you tomorrow."

Next day the queen tried some funny names she had thought of: she tried Lackland, and Chawbacon, and Clodhopper.

But none of them was right either.

"Dear, dear, you must do better than this tomorrow," the little man said. "Now you've only got three chances left."

The queen was in despair, but that night, while she was trying to think of what the little man's name could possibly be, the king came back from hunting. The queen had always been afraid to tell him anything about the straw and the little man, so he didn't know the danger his son was in.

"Such a funny thing happened to me today," he said. "I was riding through the forest when I heard someone singing. He had such an odd voice that I went to find out who it was. And it turned out to be the funniest, smallest little man I ever saw. I kept well out of sight, as you can imagine, and he didn't know I could see him. He was dancing round and round in circles, singing:

"'Today I'll brew
   Tomorrow bake,
   A little baby I'm going to take.
   For I have no kith and I have no kin –
   And my name is Rumpelstiltskin!'"

In that moment the queen began to smile, then to laugh, and then to laugh until the tears ran down her cheeks.

Quickly she told her husband the whole story. And because he was really a good man, even if a rather greedy one, he forgave her. In fact *he* laughed until he cried, too.

Next day, when the little man came on his third and last visit, instead of finding the queen all alone, she was with her husband and all the lords and ladies of the court. Of course, so as not to give the game away, they all pretended to be very gloomy, so the little man didn't have the slightest idea that the queen knew his secret.

"Now you have just three guesses left," he said, rubbing his hands together.

"Very well, is your name Zachary?"

"No!"

"Then is it Jubal?"

"No, wrong again!"

"Yes. Well, in that case, your name is RUMPELSTILTSKIN!"

The little man went deathly white.

"What . . . wha-at did you say?"

Then the king and the queen and all the court shouted out "RUMPELSTILTSKIN!"

The little man screeched with rage, jumped up and down, and rushed headlong from the room.

SMASH! He ran so fast and so furiously that he went straight through a door without opening it, and was never seen again.

The Scavenger Hunt

Joanna, Mark, and Timothy were staying in the country with their Aunt Mary. The three children enjoyed going to her house, partly because there were lots of places to play, but mostly because she had plenty of ideas for exciting games.

One day, just after lunch, it began to rain; and it looked like an unsettled afternoon. The children were disappointed, as they had planned to go off on their bicycles for a picnic. Aunt Mary saw them staring gloomily out the window.

"Never mind," she said. "You can always go out some other time. I can't do the gardening that I'd planned this afternoon either, so let's make the best of it and play an indoor game. What about a scavenger hunt?"

"Oh, yes!" exclaimed the children, who had played it several times before at Aunt Mary's.

"But this time, since you're older, we'll do it a bit differently," went on Aunt Mary. "Instead of my telling you which odd objects to go and find, this time I'll just describe something, and the one who brings back the most unusual thing that fits the description will win a point."

Young Timothy looked a bit puzzled.

"It's like this, Tim," explained Mark. "If Aunt Mary says to find something cold and wet, for instance, you might bring back a rag, or a toad, perhaps."

"I certainly wouldn't bring a toad," said Joanna, frowning.

"It sounds like a great game," said Timothy. "What's the first description?"

Aunt Mary thought for a moment. "The first thing to find is something that's yellow and slippery. Off you go!"

"Yellow and slippery." The three children dashed off in search. It was difficult.

Mark decided it was no good just rushing about the house looking. It was best to think of something that fitted the description first. "Ah! got it!" he thought, and ran down to the kitchen.

Timothy was lucky. He spied just the thing in his bedroom.

Joanna found her object in the hall.

The three children came back, each triumphant, and held out their booty to Aunt Mary.

In Mark's palm was a half-melted, sticky lump of yellow butter.

Joanna was carrying her yellow plastic raincoat. Timothy had come in very cautiously and slowly, for he was carrying a heavy bowl of goldfish.

Aunt Mary laughed. "Well, I think Tim should win this one! Especially since it isn't very easy to carry! All right, leave those things here and we'll put them back later. One point for Tim. Now try this one. Find something long and curly!"

Mark had already made up his mind that the kitchen was a good source of objects, so back he went. He found what he wanted in a drawer.

Timothy found his object in the waste-paper basket.

Joanna, much to her aunt's surprise, didn't leave the room at all. She just sat and waited for her brothers to come back, smiling to herself.

"Well then?" said Aunt Mary, when they returned.

"This is mine," announced Timothy, holding out a piece of string.

"I've got a corkscrew," said Mark.

"And what's yours, Joanna?" asked Aunt Mary. "You didn't even go out of the room."

"Here," replied Joanna, and plucked out one of her long blonde hairs.

"Splendid!" said her aunt. "That's easily the best! Come on, Mark, we'll make this one the last, and you see if you can win. Number three – find something that's difficult to see."

This time, Timothy was the only one to leave the room. When he came back, his fist was tightly clenched.

"It's an ant!" he explained, opening his hand. "Or it was – but I think it's escaped and crawled up my arm."

Joanna made a face. "Mine's not alive, thank goodness!" she said, and picked up a speck of fluff from the carpet.

"And yours, Mark?" asked Aunt Mary.

Mark held out his hand. It was empty, or if it wasn't, he was certainly holding something very difficult to see indeed.

"What is it?" asked Timothy, squinting his eyes.

"You're cheating! I can't see anything at all," said Joanna.

"It's air!" explained Mark. "Air is very difficult to see, obviously!"

"Oh, very good indeed, Mark!" laughed his aunt. "Well now, you've all won one each. But I just realized that there's one more thing to look for, after all. What's round and golden and hot?"

That was easy. The children rushed to the window.

"The sun! It's out after all!"

"I think you'll be all right for your picnic now," said their aunt. "Off you go!"

Pirate Billy and his mates have been on an interesting treasure hunt. Besides a chest full of gold they've picked up some very ordinary things that you probably have in your own house. Can you find them?

(*Answers on page 156*)

TREASURE HUNT

Playgroup

It was Susan's first day at the playgroup. She did not want to go. Her mother had said that there would be lots of other children there. Perhaps they would not play with her.

They went into a big house. In a room downstairs, lots of children were playing and running about. Two ladies were looking after them.

One of the ladies saw Susan and her mother.

"Hello," she said. "I'm Mrs. Brown. Say good-by to Mother, and come and play."

Susan's mother kissed her good-by.

"I'll come to get you after lunch. Be good."

Susan watched her go.

"What would you like to play with?" asked Mrs. Brown.

Susan looked around.

"In the sand," she said.

Mrs. Brown took her hand, and they went to the sandbox. Two boys and a girl were playing there.

"Mark and Peter and Mary," said Mrs. Brown, "Susan is new. Look after her, won't you?"

"I will, " said Mary. "Come and help us. We're putting all the sand into this bucket."

Susan used a blue cup to pick up the sand and fill the bucket. Soon it was full.

Then Mrs. Brown called, "Story time."

Mary said, "Come and sit over here."

She and Susan sat together to hear the story.

It was about a rabbit.

When it was over, Mary said, "Shall we do some painting?" Susan said yes. Mark and Michael were playing with the train set. The other children had paper to cut or dolls to play with. Susan liked painting best.

"I think I'll paint a house," said Susan.

"I'm going to paint you," said Mary.

They worked hard until lunch time. Susan looked at Mary's picture. "Is that me?" she asked.

"Yes," said Mary. "You can take it home, if you like."

After lunch all the mothers came for the children.

"Did you like it?" asked Susan's mother.

"Oh, yes!" said Susan. "I've been painting with Mary. And tomorrow we're going to play in the playhouse. Oh, yes, I liked it!"

"I knew you would," said her mother.

The Flyaway Puppet

Sidney was a glove puppet. He belonged to a boy named Bill. Sid – as he was usually called – was Bill's best-loved toy.

Bill took Sid everywhere, wearing him on his hand like a glove. He could make Sid wave his arms, nod his head, and even waggle his ears.

One day Bill's mother gave him a big, yellow balloon. It was filled with gas, so it floated high in the air.

"Hold tight to the string," she said. "If you let go of it, the balloon will fly away."

Bill had a good idea. He tied the balloon string to Sid's arm. Then he put Sid on his hand. It looked just as if Sid were holding the balloon.

Sid was glad that Bill was holding him tight. He could feel the balloon tugging on his arm, trying to pull him away.

Bill ran out to the park, where his friends were playing. "Look at this!" he shouted. He waved Sid above his head, showing him off. He forgot to hold on tight.

Whoosh! A wind blew down and tugged at the balloon. The balloon tugged at its string, and the string tugged at Sid. It pulled him from Bill's hand!

Zoom! Up high flew the balloon, taking Sid with it. "Oooo," he wailed.

He looked down. The ground was a long way away. He saw Bill, running and shouting. Bill looked very small, way down there.

The wind took Sid over the town and out over the country. Bill came running after. He came to a stream, but that didn't stop him. He ran straight through it – splish, splash! His feet were soaking wet, but he didn't notice.

Bill ran till he couldn't run another step. Then he just had to stop. He fell to the ground, feeling very weary, and very sad too. "I'll never see dear old Sid again," he thought. He felt like crying.

Sid saw Bill fall down. Then the wind blew him over a hill. "I'm lost. I'll never see dear old Bill again," he thought. He felt like crying.

But then along came a bluebird. He flew round and round the balloon, and round and round Sid. "I've never seen an airborne puppet before," he said. "Are you enjoying the ride?"

"No, I'm not!" cried Sid. "It's all an accident, and I'm so afraid of falling, and I'll never see Bill again!"

"Don't worry!" chirped the bluebird. "I'll help you." He flew at the balloon and struck it with his sharp beak.

BANG! It broke. Down fell Sid.

"Help! Do you call that helping, making me fall?" cried Sid as he dropped.

"Don't worry!" sang the bluebird. He swooped down and caught Sid as he fell. Then he landed and set Sid down.

"Thanks for saving me," said Sid. "But I have another problem. Will you help me?"

"Certainly, if I can," said the helpful bluebird. "What do you want?"

"Well," said Sid, "I'd like to get back to Bill. But I can't walk, for you can see I have no legs. Will you take me to him? He's over on the other side of the hill, and he can't see me here."

"Of course I can do that," said the bluebird. He picked up Sid – who was quite heavy for a bird to carry – and began to fly. He had to fly in circles, round and round, before he could get as high as the hill. But at last he made it over the top of the hill.

On the other side they found Bill.

The bluebird flew down low, just above Bill, and dropped Sid on Bill's head.

"What's that?" shouted Bill, jumping up, very surprised. He snatched Sid from his head, and then he saw who it was!

My, he *was* happy to see old Sid again! He put Sid on his hand, and held him very tight. He waved Sid to the bluebird, who was flying around above. "Thank you, bluebird," called Bill.

The friendly bluebird dipped his wings – the way an aircraft signals – and then he flew off. He felt happy because he'd done such a good deed for the day.

Bill and Sid were happy, too. And after that, Bill took very good care not to tie Sid to any more balloons.

You will need: material, glue or needle and thread, two buttons, one large bead, length of heavy knitting yarn

1. **Body** – Make a paper pattern by copying the drawing below. Pin it onto the material and cut out two mouse body shapes. Stick or sew the two bodies together where the drawing below is shaded at edges.

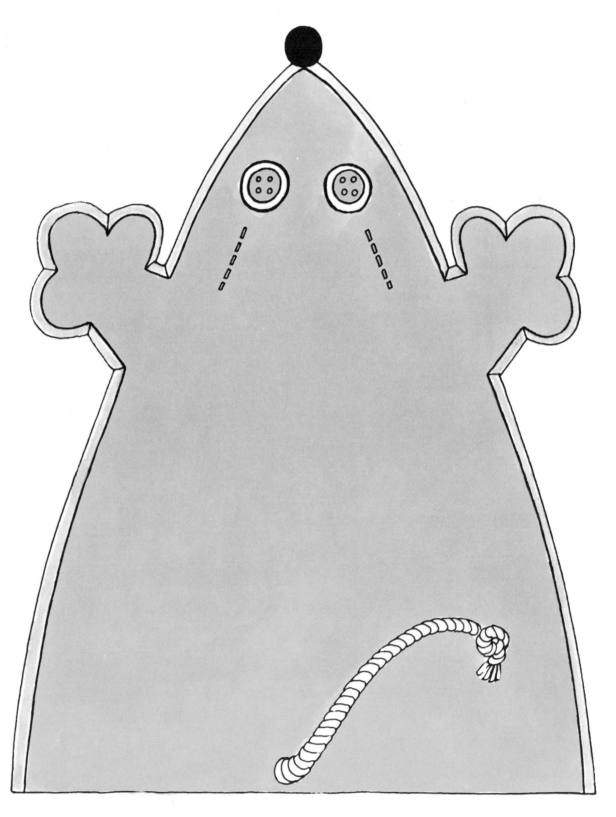

Making a Glove Puppet

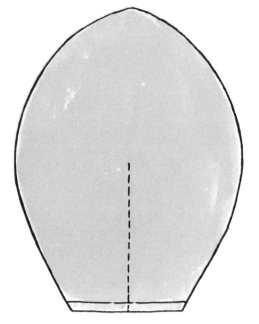

2. **Ears** – Make a pattern for the ears and cut two in felt or other material. Fold on the dotted line and glue or sew along the shaded line. The ears are glued or sewn on the body where the dotted line is.

3. **Eyes** – Sew on two buttons for the eyes.

4. **Nose** – Sew a bead on the point for nose.

5. **Tail** – Tie a knot in the yarn and sew the other end to one side of the body.

SPACE RACE

You will need: a different-colored counter for each player, spinner (see page 156)
This is a game for any number of players. Take turns spinning the spinner and moving your counters round the board. If you land on a Star, follow the trail to the rocket and continue playing from there. You must spin the exact number to finish. The first player to land on the Moon is the winner.

miss one turn

extra turn

extra turn

miss one turn

START

FINISH

extra turn

miss one turn

miss one turn

extra turn

miss one turn

extra turn

Lucky Lukmik

Lukmik was a small Eskimo boy who lived beside the frozen sea in the far Canadian north. In the winter, his house was an igloo, made from blocks of snow. His mother, father, grandmother, grandfather, aunt, uncle, cousin, and little sister lived there too. It was rather crowded in the igloo, but no one minded.

Their husky dogs lived in the snow outside the igloo, but they didn't mind that either. The dogs had very thick coats. When it was cold, they burrowed under the snow. They curled their bushy tails over their noses, and stayed quite warm.

When it wasn't snowing and blowing, the men went hunting. The dogs went with them, pulling the sled. They caught seals and walrus, and brought them home on the sled. Once they caught a polar bear!

They wouldn't take Lukmik hunting. "You're too small," said his father.

But sometimes, when they went fishing, they took Lukmik. They walked out over the frozen sea. They cut holes in the ice, and fished through the holes. Lukmik always caught lots of fish.

"I'm sure I could catch seals and walrus too, if only my father would take me hunting," thought Lukmik. While he waited to grow bigger, he made himself a hunting spear. Its shaft was cut from a piece of tree which he'd found floating on the sea last summer. Wood was very precious in Lukmik's family, because no trees grew in their country. Only small plants and mosses grew there.

The head of Lukmik's spear was made from a piece of bone. He carved and shaped it very carefully, in the old way that his father had shown him.

Lukmik was very proud of his spear. Every day, when it wasn't snowing or blowing, he took it outside the igloo. He taught himself to throw it a long way, and he always hit what he aimed at. But, as he had only snowdrifts to aim at, he never caught anything with it.

In the spring, the sun began to melt all the snow and ice. It soon melted their igloo home, too.

"It's time to hunt the caribou," said Lukmik's father. So they packed up all their belongings. Everyone had a pack to carry. Even the dogs carried packs, strapped over their backs.

They left the sea, where the thick ice was breaking up into floes and icebergs. It wasn't safe to walk on the ice any more.

They moved away from the sea, across the flat tundra land, where the snow was fast melting. Green plants and flowers were springing up everywhere. It was beautiful then, in the short, sunny summer.

The family walked a long way, for many days, across their beautiful land. At night, they unpacked their tent and slept in it. The tent was made from seal skins, sewn together by the women.

When they reached caribou country, they made camp beside a stream. In the morning, they left the tent standing. The men took their spears and went hunting. They wouldn't let Lukmik go with them. "You're still too small," they said.

Lukmik didn't like that. He didn't want to stay with the women and the baby. He wished he would hurry and grow as big as his big cousin. The men always let his cousin go hunting with them.

He took his spear and walked a short way from the tent. He sat on a rock and dreamed of being a great hunter one day.

Suddenly, a hare bounded past the rock. Quick as lightning, Lukmik threw his spear and caught the hare!

When the men came back, they were unhappy because they had found no caribou. Lukmik proudly showed them his hare.

"You're the best hunter here today!" said Lukmik's father.

Next day, they took Lukmik with them to hunt. They caught many caribou but they never took more than they needed for food and clothing.

"Lukmik brings good fortune on the hunt," said the hunters. "Let him come hunting with us every day."

After that, Lukmik always went with the hunters, and the hunting was good. They called him Lucky Lukmik.

Things to Make with Boxes
1. an aquarium

You will need: large empty box, needle and thread, scissors, paints or crayons, pebbles and shells, thin card or stiff paper, green modeling clay

1. Color the inside of the box blue, except one long side which should be the sandy color of the sea-bed.
Paint some plants around the sides.

2. Cut out some cardboard plants, bending back the bottoms to make stands.

3. Wind some green paper around a pencil and then slip it off and cut it as below. Pull the middle of the paper up and pull down the separate leaves. Glue or tape these to the tank.

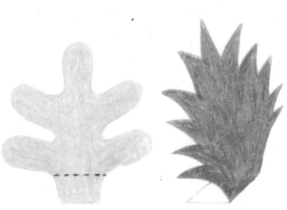

4. On the card or paper draw some fish and other sea-creatures, remembering the size of the aquarium! Cut them out carefully, and color them on both sides.

5. To make an octopus use green modeling clay for tentacles and add a ping-pong ball on top, painting it green, too.

6. To make an eel, cut a round piece of paper and then cut it as we have done, pulling the middle up to make a spiral. Paint it purple and give it a face. You can make a crab and worms from clay.

7. Using a needle and thread suspend the fish from the top of the aquarium, making good, secure knots. Put them at different heights so that they hang freely.

2. box games

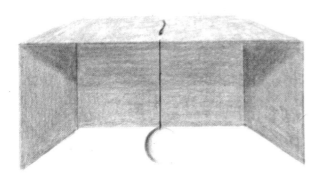

You will need: box, scissors, paint, marbles
Use a deep box lid or a box with the bottom cut out. Cut half circles of different sizes from the edge. The smallest should be big enough to let a marble through. Paint numbers over the holes. The smallest hole should have the biggest number and the biggest hole should have the smallest. Now try rolling marbles at the box and see how many points you can get in three turns. Play this game with your friends.

You will need: ping-pong ball, box, needle and thread, marbles
With a long needle, pull some thread right through the ball and knot it. Maybe a grown-up could help you with this. Tie the ball to the box so that it just touches the floor and swings freely. Aim your marbles at the ball and score one point every time you hit it.

The Lost City

Jonathan looked out from the airplane window and could see his mother and his sister Susan in her new yellow dress.

They were waving from the airport roof, a long way below, and when he could not see them any more he looked around at the other people traveling to Australia with him.

Most of them were older people, except one little girl of about eight, and as Jonathan was a year older he decided he would look after her when they landed at the airports.

He wondered if she were visiting her grandmother too, and while he was thinking about his holiday he leaned back in the comfortable seat. As the plane sped smoothly through the sky he fell fast asleep.

It was very quiet when he woke up. Then he heard one of the engines spluttering, and Jonathan knew something was wrong.

He saw the stewardess waking people and telling them to put on their safety belts.

The little girl looked very frightened, so Jonathan waved at her. After all, he was older and must not let her think that he was frightened.

Shortly afterwards the engine stopped altogether and they heard the captain say that they would have to find somewhere to land, as they would not be able to reach the next airport.

It was just getting light and Jonathan could see trees for miles in all directions, with a river running through them and some open spaces beside it. There were no towns and no lights anywhere.

The pilot was wonderful. He landed on a tiny strip of grass between the huge trees and the wide, racing river. Everyone was safe, and the stewardess served drinks and sandwiches. She told Jonathan that the radio was working and help was coming.

"We shall be here for several hours," she said. "They will have to send a boat up the river to get us."

"I don't want to sit in the airplane all day," said Jonathan, and he asked if he could look around outside.

The two children and some of the men climbed down from the plane and walked around the place where they had landed.

They had not gone far when they found a wide, flat piece of grass, leading straight from the edge of the river into the jungle.

"That looks like a road," said one of the men, "but it has not been used for a great many years."

"Let's see where it goes," said Jonathan.

They followed it into the forest and had not gone far when they saw an enormous building right in front of them.

The walls were cracked and the roof had fallen in, and great trees grew up from the floors. Through the gaps in the walls they could see other buildings, hidden among trees and bushes, and with wonderful carvings on the walls.

"A lost city," said one of the men. "No one has been here for hundreds of years."

They started to explore it right away, while some of the men went back to the plane to get their cameras.

Very soon the rest of the passengers arrived and they started to search the great buildings and the roads that led among them.

They went into the houses, which had great staircases made of carved stones, and admired the walls, which were covered with tiles in all sorts of beautiful colors.

Some of the houses had gardens with walls around them, and a lake in the middle, and the gardens were full of flowers, with butterflies and hummingbirds flitting among them.

There were temples with big, golden statues inside, and huge baths with marble sides and lovely carved stone seats.

They were still exploring the city when the boat came chugging up the river to take them away.

Jonathan thought the city was wonderful, and he did not want to leave. As the boat sailed away he was very sad.

But he vowed that one day, when he is older, he is going back to finish exploring the lost city that he found.

Mobiles to Make
A Spiral Mobile

You will need: pencil, thick card, aluminum foil, needle and thread

To make a big mobile turn a dinner plate upside down, put it on the card, and draw around it. If you would rather make a smaller mobile draw around a cup or small can. Now cut the circle out, and draw a spiral onto the card, leaving a round piece in the middle. Paint the card a different

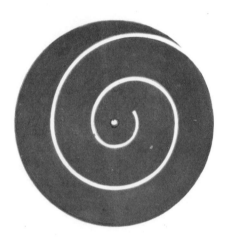

color on each side. Cut along the spiral line you have drawn.
Draw a star on card, paint it, and cut around it. Put thread through the top point, and tie it to the top of the spiral.

Cut out circles of foil. Hang these around the spiral on thread as above. You can make other shapes instead.
Insert thread through the center point of the spiral and hang it up. Perhaps you could attach it to the top of your window sill or to a shelf with sticky tape.

108

A Bird Mobile

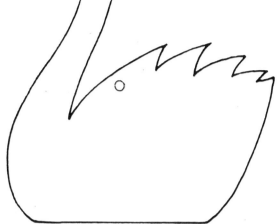

You will need: pencil, card, paint, needle and thread, plastic straws

Draw a big swan and some baby swans, a butterfly, and a bird on thick card. Trace the shapes shown here if you like. Paint them and carefully cut them out. Make holes for hanging with the point of a pencil or with the needle.

Tie the swan and the two babies onto one straw with thread and the butterfly and bird on the other. Now tie these two straws on the third with thread as shown. You will need to balance them carefully until they swing around without tipping up. Tie a long piece of thread to the middle of the whole mobile, and ask one of your parents to help you find a place to hang it.

Fables from Aesop

The Fox and the Grapes

A hungry fox was looking everywhere for something to eat. He saw some fat purple grapes growing on a trellis.

"Just what I wanted!" cried the fox. He tried to eat the grapes. But they were high above his head, and he couldn't reach them.

The fox jumped and jumped, but he still couldn't reach the grapes. At last he was too tired to jump any more.

"I didn't really want the grapes. They were probably sour anyway," he said. *It is false comfort to pretend that what we can't have is not worth having.*

The Hare and the Tortoise

A hare, who was very proud of his speedy running, teased a tortoise because she moved so slowly. But the tortoise said: "I could beat you in a race!"
The hare laughed at the tortoise. "First

one to reach the stream wins the race," he said. He sat down and watched the tortoise start slowly away.

The hare was sure that the tortoise would take a very long time to reach the stream. So he had a little snooze before he set off.

The hare woke up and raced to the stream, sure that he'd arrive before the tortoise. But she was already there. *Slow but steady is sure to win.*

The New Chair

One day Mrs. Brown was cleaning her house.

"That chair is very old," she said, looking at her armchair. "I will see if I can buy a new one."

She looked in the newspaper. There were three places which had chairs for sale.

Mrs. Brown put on her hat. She went to the first house which had a chair for sale.

A woman opened the door.

"Good morning," said Mrs. Brown. "I have come to see the chair you have for sale."

"Do come in," said the woman. "The chair is in here."

Mrs. Brown looked at the chair. It was a very big one.

"I am sorry," she said, "but this chair would be far too big for my little room."

She walked along to the next house. A man showed her in.

"I have come about the chair," she said.

"This is the one," said the man.

Mrs. Brown looked at it. This one was not too big, but it was green.

"I am sorry," said Mrs. Brown. "This would not look nice in my room. I would like a red one. Good-bye and thank you."

Mrs. Brown went on to the next house. A girl opened the door.

"Good morning," said Mrs. Brown. "May I see the chair you have for sale?"

"Oh yes," said the girl. "Come in."

Mrs. Brown looked at the chair. It was just right. It was not too big, and it was red.

"I would like to buy it," she said, and gave the girl the money.

"Will you take it now?" asked the girl.

Oh, dear! Mrs. Brown had no way of getting the chair home. She had no car. It was too big to put on the bus. What could she do?

She looked at the chair, thinking. Then she saw that on its legs were little wheels. She could push it home! The girl helped her to get it through the door. Then Mrs. Brown pushed the chair along the streets. Everyone looked at her.

Mrs. Brown just smiled. She had her chair.

A Wonderful Costume Party

It was Jeannie's birthday, and she was having a special party. All her friends were coming, in fancy dress. It was a costume party.

Jeannie dressed up as a flower seller. She wore a long red skirt and a white blouse. Over them she put a lacy black shawl. She fastened it at the front with her grandmother's big, old-fashioned brooch. On her head she wore a straw hat.

When she was ready, Jeannie took a basket to the garden. She picked some pretty flowers to fill the basket. Then she looked just like a flower seller.

The day was warm and sunshiny, for it was the middle of summer. Jeannie thought it would be lovely to have her party in the garden. She asked her mother, "Can we put the table on the grass, and have all the food out there?"

"It might rain, and that would ruin all the food," said her mother. "Let's see."

They went outdoors and looked at the sky. It was bright blue all over, with not a cloud in sight. "I'm sure it won't rain," Jeannie said.

So they took the table and chairs and food into the garden. When the table was set, it looked so good that Jeannie could hardly wait for her friends to come. She wanted to start eating the sandwiches and hot dogs, the fruit and jelly, and especially her big birthday cake.

Then her friends came. First was Walter, who was dressed as a pirate. Behind him came William and Mary, who were wearing crowns and long cloaks because they were playing king and queen.

Nora wore a big pair of glasses and carried a pile of books, to make her look like a school-teacher. Everyone could see that Dick was a horse-riding jockey, for he wore

a suit of bright red and white satin, with long black boots and a peaked cap.

Susan came as a nurse, and her brother James was a doctor. Bobby was a tennis player, all in white, with a tennis racket, too. And, last of all, in danced Grace, wearing a Hawaiian grass skirt and lots of flowers.

All her friends brought presents for Jeannie. She opened them at once, and thanked everyone. Then she asked her mother, "Is it time to eat yet?" She was really feeling very hungry.

But they played games first, so that everyone could show off his costume.

At last Jeannie's mother said, "Now it's time to eat."

But just as they were sitting down to the birthday feast – splish, splash! It started to rain! It rained so hard, they had to run into the house. The food was left behind, and was soon soaked with rain. Even the birthday cake was ruined.

Jeannie began to cry. "Oh, I wish it weren't raining!" she sobbed.

Then another girl popped into the room. She looked just like a fairy, with long golden hair, a pretty short skirt, lovely wings, and a magic wand. Actually, she wasn't a girl at all. She *was* a fairy!

"I'm the birthday-wish fairy," she told Jeannie. "I can't stop the rain falling here, but I can take you to a place where it isn't raining!"

She waved her wand, and quick as a wink, they were in fairyland. The sun was shining, of course, for it never stops shining there. And waiting for the children was a beautiful birthday picnic. It was even better than the feast that the rain ruined. The hungry children sat down at once, and ate as much as they wanted. Then they went exploring, all over fairyland.

They met plenty of fairies, and elves and dwarfs, too. They saw some beautiful sights, and the chief magician of all fairyland put on a magic show for them.

What a wonderful costume party!

Making Costumes

Martian

A Martian wears short trousers or a short skirt, and a shirt or blouse back to front – with the buttons up the back. To make the hat, find a square cardboard box whose sides measure approximately 8 inches. Cut away one side (and the lid if there is one) so that the box will fit on your head like a square hat. Now open four plastic egg boxes and lay them flat. Glue one egg box to each side of the cardboard box.
Use knitting needles for the antennae. Make 2 small holes in the egg box on the top of the hat and push the pointed ends of the needles through. Use sticky tape to hold them in place.

Scarecrow

A scarecrow wears tattered clothes – very raggedy and too big for him. He has straw sticking out of his cuffs, a funny painted face, and a battered old hat.

Grand Lady

A grand lady wears a very large, droopy hat. Round her hat is a long scarf, with its ends trailing down her back. She has lots and lots of beads, and a long skirt.

Indian Chief

An Indian chief wears anything he likes, but on top he always wears a blanket. Round his head is a band of cloth, with some feathers sewn to it. He has bright warpaint on his face.

Hawaiian Dancer

A Hawaiian dancer wears a grass skirt and leis (necklaces) of flowers. Here's how you can make them.

For the grass skirt you will need: brown wrapping paper, sticky tape, and scissors

1. The paper should be wide enough to reach from your waist to your knees, and long enough to go round your waist twice. If your paper isn't long enough, fasten on another piece with sticky tape.
2. Make cuts, ½ inch apart, all along the paper, leaving 3 inches uncut along the top, for the waistband.
3. Wrap the skirt around your waist, and fasten it in place with sticky tape.

For the leis you will need: colored paper, sticky tape, scissors, needle and thread

1. Cut the paper in strips, 2 inches wide. Make a sandwich of about four strips, so you can cut them out all together. Cut out petal shapes (see diagram). With thin paper, you'll need about 24 petals for each flower.
2. Lay down a 5 inch strip of sticky tape, sticky side up. Lay the pointed ends of the petals on the tape, overlapping them. Roll up the sticky tape tightly, and the flower is made.
3. Make about 15 or 20 flowers. String them together by their sticky tape ends, using a strong needle and heavy thread or string. Tie the ends of the string together.
4. You can make flower wreaths for your hair and flower bracelets in the same way.

119

Dunstable Pig

Dunstable Pig was the only pig on Farmer Green's farm, deep down in the country. It was a happy farmyard, for all the animals were very gregarious, and Farmer Green treated them like members of his family. Dunstable was a cheery creature. He spent his days wallowing in his muddy sty and rooting for his food in the trough which he shared with the chickens.

One day, the chickens were surprised to see that Dunstable Pig did not appear at feeding-time. Instead of greedily eating all the food themselves in his absence, some of them went, in their kind-hearted way, to find out why Dunstable was in his sty.

Dunstable's pink snout drooped.

"I'm not feeling quite myself," he grunted. "No, I mean I am feeling myself and I don't like it."

"What a complicated thing to say," said the chickens. "You're talking nonsense, just like when you ate all those fermented apples last autumn."

"I'm not drunk," Dunstable snorted. "What I was trying to say was simple enough. I don't like being a pig."

"Not like being a pig?" clucked the chickens in chorus. "Why not?"

"It's my tail!" burst out Dunstable. "I can't think why I never noticed it before – I'm the only animal on the farm with a curly tail, and I do feel like a fool."

The chickens turned their round eyes towards Dunstable's plump hindparts. His tail was indeed as curly as a corkscrew. Dunstable, embarrassed, shuffled into a corner of his sty to conceal it. A chicken chuckled, "I say, I could try to straighten it out for you, if you're really upset about it. I'll give it a sharp pull in my beak."

Dunstable, half eager and half fearful, turned around and proffered his tail. The chicken grabbed it in his beak and tugged. Dunstable gave a loud squeak of pain and tweaked his tail abruptly away. The chicken lost his balance and fell into the mud of Dunstable's sty.

"That hurt," moaned Dunstable, as the disgruntled chicken picked himself up and dusted his feathers. "There must be an easier way."

"What about tying your tail to the gate and then walking forwards?" put in the farm cat, whose curiosity had brought him over. "I'll fetch a piece of string from the barn."

Dunstable's tail was attached to the gate in a very professional granny-knot. He took one step forward, then a second. He tugged and strained. His tail stretched a little, but at once sprung back into shape whenever Dunstable paused for breath.

"It's no good trying to stretch it straight," Dunstable realized. "It has to be flattened."

"Shall I try sitting on it?" suggested the horse.

"Thank you all the same," said Dunstable, well aware of the size of the horse, "I'd rather not."

Farmer Green's collie had another idea. "What about putting it between two bricks?"

Dunstable passed a very uncomfortable

night with his tail fixed between the heavy bricks. At daybreak, tired, and with an aching back, he extracted his tail. After all that discomfort, it was as twisted as ever. "I believe it's even curlier," thought Dunstable in despair.

He meandered over to the pond to have his bath. An early duck was diving.

"You look very gloomy," observed the duck, shaking the water from his eyes.

"I've suffered all night from a clamped tail," explained Dunstable. "I was trying to straighten it, but it hasn't worked."

"Water is the thing to take out kinks," said the duck. "Why don't you sit on the bank and dangle your tail into the pond?"

Dunstable Pig missed two mealtimes through sitting with his tail in the water. At suppertime, he could bear it no longer; he was wet, cold, and starving.

The chickens had given him up and had almost finished the food. Dunstable tucked in greedily, but after a few mouthfuls, he lost his appetite. He felt a chill in every bone, and his snout was running. His tail was sopping wet and very bedraggled, but it curled as obstinately as before. He crept, despondent and dreary, into the far corner of his pen. No one could cheer him up.

Farmer Green was worried by Dunstable's strange behavior, not knowing the cause of it. He decided that Dunstable needed a change of scene. Next morning, he led Dunstable across the farmyard, through the five-barred gate, and into an empty paddock.

Dunstable wandered glumly around. Suddenly, he noticed figures in the next field, which belonged to the neighboring farm. Some other pigs, the first of his kind which Dunstable had ever seen, were exercising there. Dunstable was horrified. Supposing they noticed his curly tail? Crouching down, he peeped furtively at them. Then he saw the back view of one pig. It had a twisty tail!

"I'm not the only one!" he squeaked.

The other pigs came across at the sound. Every single one had a curly tail!

Light dawned on Dunstable Pig.

"How stupid I've been! All pigs have curly tails! Curly tails are our sign, our special sign of piggishness! Curly tails are to be carried with pride!"

SHADOW PUPPETS

Here are some animals you can make with just your hands. Find a light that makes good strong shadows on the wall or on a piece of white paper, then see how many of these beasts you can bring to life. You must stand between the light and the wall or paper.

Camel

Rabbit

Pig

Teddy Bear

Antelope

Terrier

Elephant

Goat

Dog begging

Fox

Goose

Bull Terrier

Bird

Llama

Feodor's Feet

Feodor was a housefly. He lived with his fly friends in Mr. Taylor's house. They were always landing with their dirty feet on any uncovered food. They all liked food which was nasty-smelling or rotten, and Feodor had a passion for raw meat. He would hang around Mr. Taylor's kitchen for hours, waiting to alight on a steak or the cat food.

Mr. Taylor knew the flies were in his kitchen, and the buzzing irritated him. He was rather careless, though, and not very good at catching the flies. The minute they landed on the ceiling, he gave up chasing them, as he was not agile enough to stand on a chair. The flies knew they were safe up there, and laughed, upside-down.

One day Feodor was enjoying a juicy pork chop when Mr. Taylor caught him at it and pounced on him with a rolled-up newspaper. Feodor escaped, and hurried to the safety of the ceiling. To his horror, he found that he could not stick to it! Again and again he landed, again and again his feet lost their grip. Flustered, he tumbled to the floor, but luckily for him, he finished up behind the sideboard, out of range of the weapon.

Mr. Taylor put away his chop and went out. Buzzing excitedly, Feodor's friends crowded round making Feodor's head hurt even more.

"I can't stick," moaned Feodor. "I land, but I can't stick! What's the future for a fly who can't suspend safely from the ceiling?"

"There must be something wrong with your suckers," said a friend. "Lie on your back and put your feet in the air so that we can examine them."

Feodor tucked in his wings and rolled over. The others peered at his six feet.

"They look normal, there's nothing broken," said one, feeling Feodor's feet.

"Then his suckers must have lost their stick!" cried another, in horror.

"I'll try massage," offered an elderly fly. "It might do the trick."

He rubbed Feodor's hairy legs until both of them were hot and bothered. But Feodor's feet grew no stickier.

"We could put glue on them," suggested another friend.

"That's no use," snapped Feodor. "I'd stick to the ceiling all right, but I'd never leave it again!"

"What about using marmalade then?" persisted his friend. "It's sticky, but not so final as glue. You'd have to keep renewing it, of course," he added.

"The marmalade's only out at breakfast time," said Feodor. "What would I do the rest of the day?"

Another plan was put forward.

"Fix a piece of cotton thread around your middle and tie it to two of us. Then we could keep you safely up on the ceiling."

"That wouldn't work," said Feodor, now

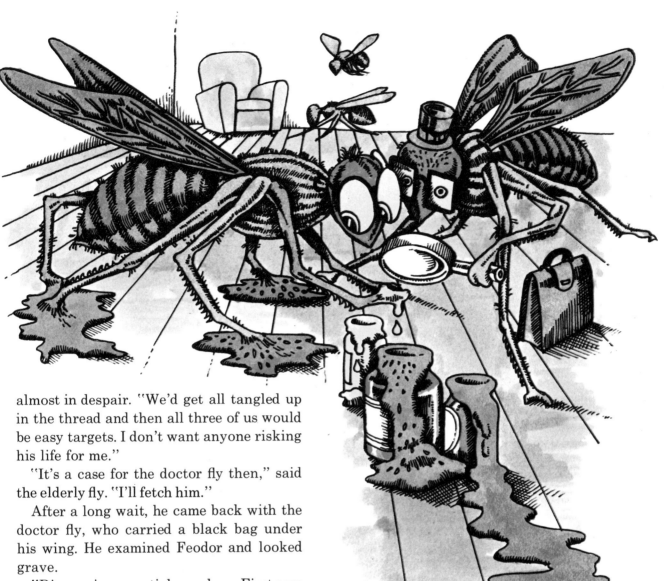

almost in despair. "We'd get all tangled up in the thread and then all three of us would be easy targets. I don't want anyone risking his life for me."

"It's a case for the doctor fly then," said the elderly fly. "I'll fetch him."

After a long wait, he came back with the doctor fly, who carried a black bag under his wing. He examined Feodor and looked grave.

"Diagnosis—non-sticky suckers. First case I've ever come across. You'll make medical history in the insect world, my lad."

"I don't care about fame," groaned Feodor. "Just tell me how I can get better!"

The doctor fly was obviously at a loss.

"Well," he pronounced, finally, "I suggest a complete rest. You've had a very bad shock. Then you must eat nothing but sticky things, and plenty of them. Find a safe place to stay, and get your friends to feed you."

Feodor settled as best he could in the back of an armchair while his friends buzzed away in their search for sticky morsels. During the course of that day and the next, Feodor ate porridge, marmalade, jam, honey, custard, condensed milk, treacle, syrup, toffee, chocolate, and even a piece of chewing gum which Mr. Taylor's nephew had dropped. Every few hours, the doctor examined his suckers. At last, he announced excitedly, "Sufficiently sticky! Hurrah!"

By now, Feodor felt rather sick, but he rallied at the prospect of trying out his newly-recovered suckers. His friends watched in mingled hope and fear as he flew higher and higher. He turned, landed, and there he stuck! He hopped off, landed again, and stuck again. He was cured! Buzzing with joy, Feodor performed a little upside-down dance. Mr. Taylor came in in the middle of Feodor's celebrations and glared at him.

"If you weren't up on that ceiling . . ." he mumbled, threateningly.

Poor Mr. Taylor. He should have known that if you don't want flies in the house you shouldn't leave food around!

Edgar and Egbert and the Jam Can

Yum! Those campers are cooking bacon.
Let's ask them for some.

No, no, don't do that! They might chase us!
But they look like friendly people . . .
I have a better idea. Come on!

What are we doing?
Ssshh! We'll sneak up behind and *take*
some food while they're not looking.

But that's *stealing*! That's not nice!
Who cares? I'm going to have this jam!

Slurp, slurp!
It *does* taste good.

Sorry I can't leave any
for you, Egbert!

Oooh, it's stuck!
Greedy fellow, Edgar.
You should have shared it!

Now we're home, I have
to eat *your* supper as well.
But I'll help you later.

I'll tug and tug and tug the can
until it comes off.
OUCH!

The Jungle Path

You will need: one counter for each player, spinner (see page 156)
Follow the jungle path, but beware of the dangers that lurk. Each player spins the spinner to determine how many squares he can move along the path. Be sure to follow directions of the squares you land on. First one out of the jungle wins.

25

FINISH
You have reached
the hunting lodge

START

1

2

You have take
the wrong turni
miss one turn

1

3

Elephants crossing
miss one turn

9

4

8

5

Rapids to cross
go back to 4

Crocodile on ban
run to 9

7

6

The Ugly Duckling

One after the other Mrs. Duck's seven chicks scurried along behind her, each one a small round ball of soft yellow and brown feathers. Each one, that is, except the seventh and last. This duckling was different. Not small, or round, or yellow and brown at all, but big, grey, and untidy.

Mrs. Duck couldn't understand him at all. He could certainly swim very well, and he really was very big for his age. But he didn't look like any of his brothers and sisters, or indeed like any other duckling Mrs. Duck had ever seen. All her friends praised the first six, but did nothing but say nasty things about the seventh.

"My dear," said one, "that ugly duckling is no child of yours, believe me!"

"I don't think he's a duckling at all," said another. "A turkey must have pushed one of its eggs among yours."

But as far as the Ugly Duckling himself was concerned, that wasn't the worst of it. As the days passed, the other animals began to bully him.

The geese started it – being bad-tempered by nature. Then the chickens began. Next it was the cats and dogs and cows. At last, even the Ugly Duckling's brothers and sisters, and Mrs. Duck herself, began to be rude to him.

Poor Ugly Duckling couldn't stand it any longer. He ran away – or rather, he swam away. As fast as he could go.

Now it wasn't really a very big river, and the further up it the Ugly Duckling swam, the smaller it became, until, in the end, it seemed to melt away in a big flat field. The ground was wet and marshy and the grass and reeds grew on all sides.

The Ugly Duckling was wondering what to do next, when two wild geese stuck their heads through the thick reeds.

"Hey, who are you?" one of them called, very rudely.

"And what are you doing here?" added the other, even more rudely.

"Please sir," the Ugly Duckling replied, "I'm a duckling – people say a very ugly one – and I've run away from home because . . . "

But at that moment, there was a loud BANG! and then another.

"HUNTERS!" cried the two geese together, and flew off, fast and low.

BANG! BANG!! BANG!!! Guns were going off all around, while the hunters' dogs barked.

The Ugly Duckling ran first one way, then the other. But wherever he went, guns roared, dogs barked, and bullets whistled overhead.

At last, the shooting stopped, and the hunters and their dogs went away.

So did the Ugly Duckling – but in the opposite direction from them. He ran as fast and as far as he could, away from the marsh. In fact, he ran until he was so tired he couldn't run another step. Then he sat down and tried to think what he should do next.

"I must find somewhere warm to spend the night," he thought to himself. He looked around. And there, a little way away, he saw a tumble-down cottage made of bits of wood, sticks, and straw. Best of all, it had a door with a small hole in the bottom.

Quickly he wriggled through.

Inside it was warm and steamy and smelled of soup. An old woman was sitting by the fire stirring a big black cooking pot. On her lap sat a black cat, and a brown hen was pecking at some grain on the floor in front of the hearth.

"Who's there?" called the old woman. "My eyes aren't as good as they used to be."

"It's only me – a duckling. An ugly duckling."

"What's that? My ears aren't as good as they used to be, either. A duck did you say? Good! Now I shall have duck eggs to eat."

Ugly Duckling tried to explain that he wasn't a lady duck and so couldn't lay eggs, but the old woman couldn't understand him.

And so, day after day, she waited for him to lay eggs. The hen and the cat waited, too,

even though Ugly Duckling told them, time after time, that he couldn't. Of course, *they* should have been able to understand him, but they didn't seem to want to.

In fact, as time passed, they all got more and more impatient with him. The cat bit him, the hen pecked him, and the old woman hit him with her broom.

So once again Ugly Duckling ran away. This time he ran until he came to a little lake among a group of trees. And there he stayed.

It was rather lonely there, for no other birds lived on the lake. There were no animals in the country round about, and hardly any fish in the water.

But Ugly Duckling didn't mind at all, because that meant there was nobody to bully him or call him names.

Autumn came. Still Ugly Duckling lived alone and saw no one. But then, one day, when the dying leaves covered the surface of the water with a beautiful carpet of gold and red and purple, he saw a whole flock of

great white birds flying high in the sky. They had long graceful necks, and though their wings seemed to be beating slowly, they were flying very fast.

Ugly Duckling called to them, but they couldn't hear him.

He tried to fly after them, but his wings were too small to lift him off the ground. So, while the great white birds flew on towards the warm south where they went for the winter, Ugly Duckling stayed behind.

Soon the days grew short, grey, and cold, the nights long and even colder. Snow fell, and the lake began to freeze, first just around the edges, then more and more, until only a tiny little circle of clear water was left in the middle. In this little circle the duckling swam around and around all night and most of every day. He was sure that if he stopped swimming the water would freeze over completely.

But then, one day, the weather changed. The wind became softer, the sun just a little warmer, and, quite suddenly, the trees were covered with green buds.

"It's Spring," sighed Ugly Duckling, and stretched. "How good!"

And he stretched again, flapped his wings, . . . and then, to his great surprise, found himself rising out of the water. He kicked out with his feet. And the next moment, he was flying. For the first time ever.

Ugly Duckling was so pleased and excited that for some time he didn't bother to look where he was going. But when he did finally look down, he saw a river below him, and on it swam three beautiful white birds, just like the ones he had seen flying away in the Autumn.

"I must find out what sort of birds they are," he said to himself. "That is, if they will speak to someone as ugly and awkward as me."

Carefully he steered himself down and landed on the river. The three white birds slowly and proudly swam towards him. They raised their heads and opened their wings . . .

"They're going to kill me! I know it!" thought the duckling. "This is their river and they don't want anyone as ugly as me on it."

He opened his wings to fly away. But then he closed them again. "No," he said. "I'm tired of running away all the time. If I am ugly, then I'm ugly, and they will just have to put up with it!"

Then he called out to the white birds: "I know I'm ugly, but I won't go away. So if you don't like me you will just have to kill me."

"Kill you? What on earth for?" answered one of the birds.

"Go away? But we don't want you to go away," said the second.

"Ugly? Who said you were ugly?" said the third. "Why, you are the most handsome swan of us all!"

"Don't be ridiculous. Everyone calls me Ugly Duckling."

"Your'e the one who is being ridiculous," cried the first bird. "You're a swan like us. If you don't beleive me, why, just look down!"

Ugly Duckling looked down at his reflection in the water. And it was true.

He wasn't grey and ugly any more! He was white and graceful and very, very beautiful. He *was* a swan!

He never ever discovered how he came to be hatched among a family of ducks. But then, it didn't really matter, did it?

EASY WEAVING

You will need: box, oddments of wool, knitting needle, card

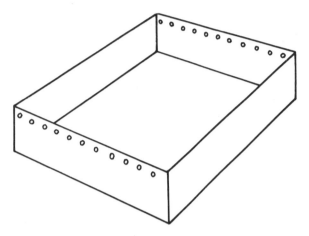

Make holes in two ends of a box with the knitting needle, as shown. Be sure to make the same number at each end.

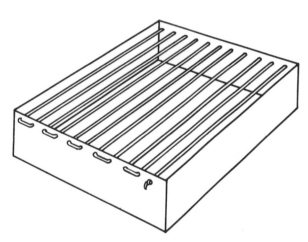

With a very long piece of wool, thread through the first hole and make a knot. Take the wool across the box and through the first hole in the other side. Now back through the second hole, and so on, to the end of the box. Make sure the threads are very tight, and finish by tying a knot. Now cut a piece of card as shown, and wind wool around it. Tie the end of the wool

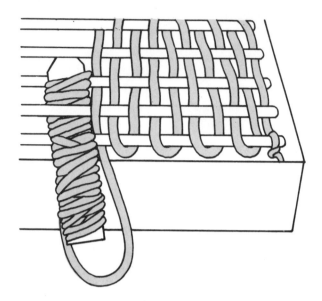

on the card to the first cross-thread on the box and push the card over and under the cross-threads as shown above. When you get to the other side, turn around and come back as shown above. Work right across the box. Do not pull the thread too tight, but

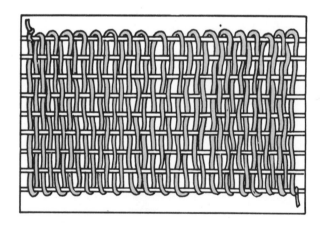

make sure you push each line close up to the last.

When you have woven all across the box, knot the wool to the last cross-thread and cut the cross-threads with the scissors so that the mat comes away from the box. You can weave several squares and sew them together to make a large, colorful mat or a doll's blanket.

MAKING POM POMS

You will need: pencil, stiff card, spool, wool, scissors

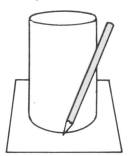 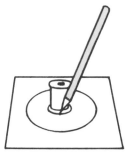

1. Draw around a small saucer on a piece of card and then put a spool as near to the center of this circle as you can and draw around it. Cut around both circles.

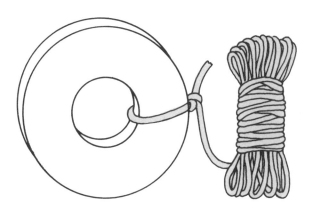

2. You will need to cut two pieces of card with holes in the center as above. Wind some wool so that it will pass through the center hole. Tie the two cards together and wind the wool around them, as shown below. Continue winding around and around like this, building up layers of wool.

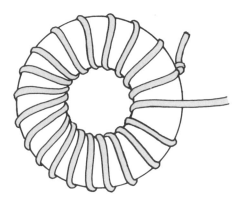

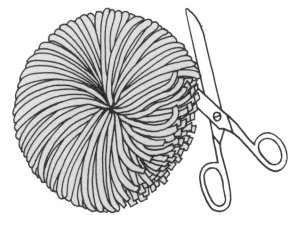

3. When you cannot get any more wool through the hole, cut the wool. Then, putting the point of the scissors between the two pieces of card, cut all around the circle in between the cards. Now slip a length of wool in between the cards and tie it as tightly as you can: do this twice to make it strong.

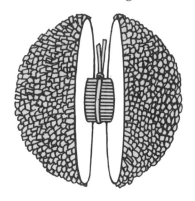

4. Now pull the cards off the wool. You can use pom poms for decorating hats, scarves, or you can tie elastic to one and make a baby's toy.

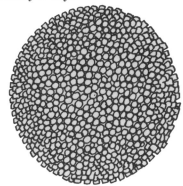

The Fruit Stall

Michael and Sally are shopping at the
fruit stall. Their mother has told them they
can have as much fruit as they like.
What would you choose? What colors are
the different fruits? How many of each
fruit are there?

The Playhouse

James and Tina were playing in the garden. It was a very hot day.

"I'm too hot to play outside," said Tina.

"Well, the baby is asleep indoors," said her brother, "so we can't play there."

"What we need is a house of our own," said Tina.

"We'll make one!" said James. "Down under the trees. I'll get some boxes, if you find something to use as a roof."

Tina ran to fetch an old tablecloth.

"We'll use the trees by the fence," said James.

"Then we can have the fence as the back of our house."

They hung the tablecloth from one tree to the other. James piled up the boxes to make walls. Tina said she wanted a big doorway. Then she could push her dolls' pram in and out. James wanted small windows. Then he could hide and fire his toy gun if someone came.

Soon, they had a box for a table and chairs from the garden shed. Tina's dolls sat all around the table. She wanted to give them their dinner. She took out her dolls' tea set. James was looking out of the window.

"Here comes Mother!" he said. "I'll make her jump with my gun."

"Bang!" went his toy gun. Their mother looked around. She saw the house at the bottom of the garden.

"What a lovely house!" she said. "May I come in, if I'm not too big?"

She went into the house and sat down.

"I was just going to give my dolls their dinner," said Tina. "Then James can wash up."

"Oh, no, I won't," said James. "I'm going to fetch my cars. I think this house would make a good garage."

"Oh, no! I want it as a house," said Tina.

"A garage!" shouted James.

"Look," said their mother, "it's such a good place, you can use it for all sorts of things. It can be a house one day, a garage the next. Then you can use it as a shop or a school or even a hospital. But if you keep it as a house for now, you can eat your own dinner in here."

And so they did.

The Bicycle

"What do you want for your birthday, John?" asked his mother.

"A bicycle, please."

"And what would you like if you can't have a bicycle?" said his father.

"I only want a bicycle."

"They cost far too much," said his father. "You will have to wait a long time before you get one. I can only afford the bell at the moment."

"That will do for a start," said John. "I will go and clean out the shed, so there will be somewhere to put it."

"He is very determined," said his sister Julia. "Do you think that if we all bought him something towards it, we could gradually get it for him?"

"That's a good idea," said her father. "Don't say anything to him, but go down to the bicycle shop and ask for a book showing all the parts of a bicycle."

Off Julia went and came home with a large colored book. Then, with her mother helping her, she cut out all the pictures showing the parts of a bicycle.

Then her father wrote some letters, her mother addressed the envelopes, and Julia put in the pictures and stuck on the stamps.

When John came in later, very grubby after clearing out the shed, they were all looking very pleased with themselves.

"What have you been doing?" he asked.

"Just writing," said Julia. "Now you go and wash off that dirt."

Nobody mentioned the bicycle again during the next week, except when John found a picture of a bicycle under a cushion in a chair. He could not understand why the bell had been cut out, but he pinned it on his bedroom wall just the same. He now had twenty-three pictures of bicycles.

He was a little bit disappointed on his birthday, as there were no presents waiting for him.

"I guess the mailman is late," said Julia.

"But there are lots of cards," he answered.

"Perhaps the packages were too heavy for him," she replied, but she had a great big grin as she said it.

"I believe you are hiding something," said John. "What is it?"

"Wait and see," said Julia. "I've got to help Mother make the cakes."

As she hurried to the kitchen, John searched the house, but there were no packages anywhere. There was nothing in the bedrooms, or in the shed, or in the tall cupboard where Mother hid the candy.

Just before lunch there was a knock at the door, and John got there first.

There was a man with a box, and it was addressed to John, but right across the top were the words:

NOT TO BE OPENED UNTIL TWO O'CLOCK.

"Why not?" said John. Just then Uncle Henry drove up. He was carrying a big square box, and right across it were the same words:

NOT TO BE OPENED UNTIL TWO O'CLOCK.

142

For the rest of the morning the parcels kept arriving. They were all addressed to John and they all had the same message: OPEN AT TWO O'CLOCK.

While he ate his lunch John kept looking at the big heap of packages on the floor. They were all shapes and sizes. Some were only as big as his hand and some were nearly big enough to get inside, but none of them could be opened until two o'clock.

He sat on the floor while his mother and sister cleared the table. He shook and felt all the packages until it was nearly two o'clock, but he still could not tell what was in them.

Then his friends and his family came into the room and his mother put an old blanket on the floor. "To pick up the mess," she said.

"I would open the small ones first," said Dad. "It is two o'clock now."

The first present was a little box from Julia, and in it was a bicycle bell.

"That is because I told her I want a bicycle one day," he said to Uncle Henry.

"Then I will be able to put this on it."

The next was a peculiar present, in a red box, from one of his twin cousins. It was a bicycle pedal. There was a blue box from the other twin. In it was another bicycle pedal.

A long, funny-shaped packet from Mother turned out to be a set of handlebars, and Daddy's big box contained a back wheel.

Uncle Henry's box held a front wheel and the rest of the presents from his aunts and grandparents contained the frame, chain, saddle, mudguards, and all the pieces for a complete bicycle.

What a mess was on the floor! No wonder Mother had put down the old blanket.

When the last package was opened, Daddy and Uncle Henry, with John helping, put all the pieces together, and when they had finished John was sitting on the finest bicycle he had ever seen.

To this day, he is certain that it is the best present he has ever had.

BOX CITY

Make the movie house from two long boxes. Put a matchbox and ping-pong ball on top of one and half an egg box on the other. Stand it on a box lid base and use a small box for a door. Decorate with corrugated paper and lettering from magazines.

You will need: various boxes and used containers, glue and paint

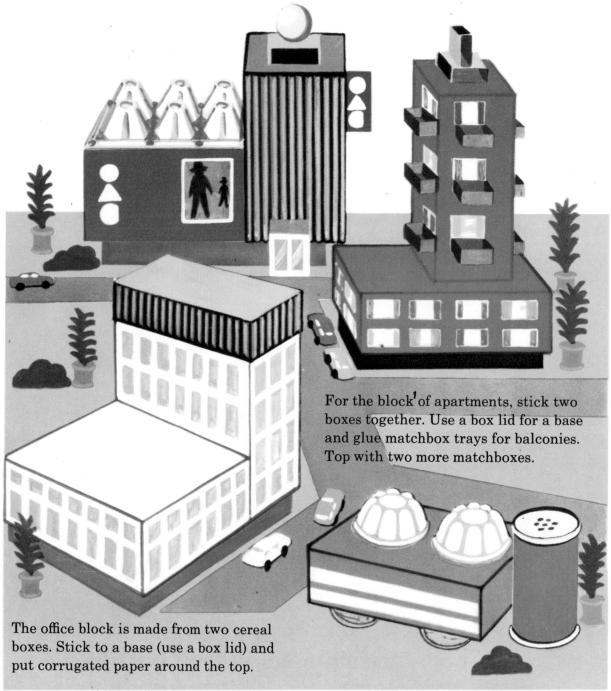

For the block of apartments, stick two boxes together. Use a box lid for a base and glue matchbox trays for balconies. Top with two more matchboxes.

The office block is made from two cereal boxes. Stick to a base (use a box lid) and put corrugated paper around the top.

Stick all the models to a base board and paint them with thick paint. Paint roads, etc., on the board and decorate with bushes made from bits of old sponge.

The exhibition hall is made from a box topped with two jelly molds. Stand the box on four sour cream cartons and stick a round container at the end for a doorway.

BOX FARM

You will need: a selection of boxes, as for the city, some lids (for fields), lots of *used* wooden matches for fences, modeling clay

The farmhouse is made from two square boxes. Cut one in half for the roof (see pages 50-51) and stick on top of the other. Make a chimney from matchboxes. Use a small box for a door.

Animals can be made from clay, as shown. Use matches for legs.

The haystack is made in the same way as the farmhouse. Paint bales of hay on the sides.

Use an old mirror for a pond and stick clay round the edges on the baseboard.

The cottage is like the farmhouse, only smaller. Make the stable in the same way and stick it onto the side of the farmhouse.

Make fields from box lids with used matches round the sides for fences. Straws can also be stuck to matches for fences. Stick all the models to a board and paint it.

145

Things to Make with Spools

Make a Train

You will need: small boxes, spools, plastic straws, matchbox, modeling clay, paints, glue

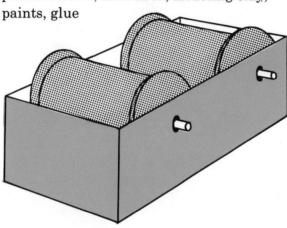

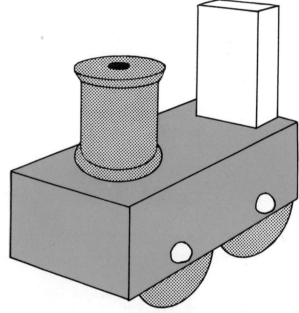

Make two small holes on either side of a little box. Make sure the holes are exactly opposite each other and big enough to push a straw through. Push a straw through one hole and then through the spool and out the other side. Cut the straw to fit.

See how it rolls along. Fix the straws with clay to keep them from slipping out. Glue a spool on top of the box as a chimney and a matchbox as a driver's cab. Paint the entire engine with thick paint.

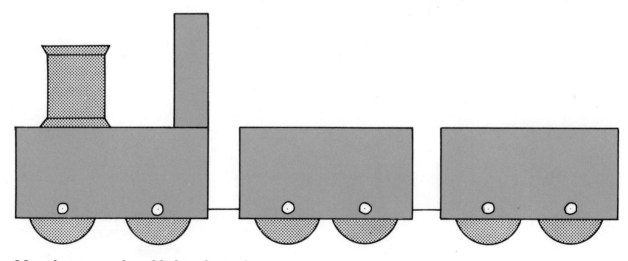

More boxes can be added to the train. Paint them in different colors. Make a small hole in each box and attach them together with string. Maybe you could make a toy train as a present for someone.

A Merry-Go-Round

You will need: 3 spools, card, long nail, piece of wood, paints, glue, needle and thread, drawing pin

Hammer a long nail into the center of a fairly small piece of wood. Glue the three spools on top of each other and place over the nail. Trace around a saucer onto card and cut around the circle. Stick this to the top of the reels with glue.

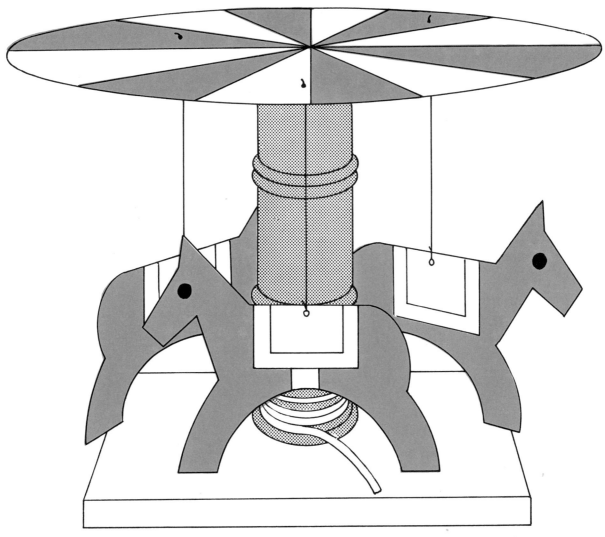

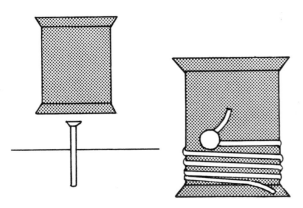

Fix a thumbtack to the bottom spool and tie some string to it. Now wind the

Draw four horses on lightweight cardboard. If you like, trace the center horse above, and use as a pattern. Paint the horses and cut them out. Using a needle and thread, punch a hole in the top of the merry-go-round, thread it through a horse, and tie it – leaving the horse enough thread to hang prettily. Hang the others in the same way.

string around the reel, leaving a bit to pull. This will make the merry-go-round move around.

Silent Night

Si-lent night! Ho-ly night! All is calm, all is bright

Round yon Virgin Moth-er and Child, Ho-ly In-fant so ten-der and mild,

Sleep in heav-en-ly peace, --- Sleep - - in heav-en-ly peace.

Silent night! Holy night!
Shepherds quake at the sight,
Glories stream from heaven afar,
Heavenly Hosts sing Alleluia;
Christ, the Saviour, is born,
Christ, the Saviour, is born.

Silent night! Holy night!
Son of God, love's pure light
Radiant beams from Thy holy face,
With the dawn of redeeming grace;
Jesus, Lord, at Thy birth,
Jesus, Lord, at Thy birth.

148

Santa Claus Loses His Reindeer

One Christmas Eve, Santa Claus was delivering his presents. A great blizzard was blowing and snowing. He could hardly see where he was going, in his big sleigh drawn by his eight reindeer.

They landed on a roof. He clambered from the sleigh and groped about in the blizzard till he bumped into the chimney.

"Tsk!" he said. "I like snow, but all this is too much! If it goes on, I'll never get to all the children tonight."

Then he slid down the chimney, into the house. He left some beautiful presents for the children who lived there.

Back he went, up the chimney, to the roof. All he could see was snow, thicker than ever. All he could hear was the wind.

"Where are you, reindeer?" he called. He listened, but he couldn't hear them. He walked over the roof with his hands stretched out, feeling for the reindeer. But he went

the wrong way and suddenly – whoosh – he fell off the edge of the roof!

Whump! He landed up to his ears in a deep snowdrift. He wasn't at all hurt, but the snow was cold, especially where it got up his sleeves and trousers.

He clambered from the snowdrift and tried to find the house. But he'd got turned round again, and he went the wrong way!

"Reindeer! Reindeer, where are you?" he called. But they didn't hear him. At last he decided to go on without them, for the presents had to be delivered. So he walked from house to house with them.

In a little shed, behind one of the houses, lived a little donkey. He was a good fellow, and he worked very hard. Santa Claus tiptoed into the shed to leave a present. But he stepped on a creaky board, and the noise woke the donkey.

"Hello, Santa Claus," said the donkey.

"Why are you covered in snow?"

"I'm walking tonight," said Santa Claus. "I've lost my reindeer."

"I'll take you around!" said the little donkey. "I'm very strong!"

Santa Claus was quite tired by then, and in a bigger hurry than ever, so he let the donkey carry him. They went together for miles, delivering presents.

At last Santa Claus said, "You must be tired, little donkey. Go home now, and thank you for all your help."

So the donkey went home.

Santa Claus walked on. At the next house, he saw an open window. "Oh good," he said. "I won't bother to go in by the chimney. I'll pop through the window."

In he went. He was just putting some presents under the tree when a man rushed into the room and jumped on him!

"Got you, you mean thief!" cried the man, whose name was Mr. Murphy.

"Me? A thief?" said Santa Claus. "Don't be silly. I'm Santa Claus, and I'm putting presents under the tree, not stealing them away! Now kindly stop sitting on my stomach, and let me go!"

Mr. Murphy leaped up and turned on the light. "Santa Claus!" he said. "Why did you climb through the window? I thought you always came down the chimney."

Santa Claus told him everything that had happened to him since he lost his reindeer. Mr. Murphy made him a pot of tea to warm his insides, and gave him a dry pair of socks to warm his wet feet.

Suddenly, they heard sleighbells. A moment later, a reindeer was looking through the window.

"There you are, Santa Claus! We've looked everywhere for you!" he said.

They were all very glad to be together again. Santa Claus thanked Mr. Murphy for the tea and socks, and then he hurried on his way.

All night long Santa Claus and his reindeer rushed around the houses. By Christmas morning, their work was done. All the children found lovely presents from Santa Claus when they woke up.

And do you know who found the very best Christmas presents that morning? The little donkey and Mr. Murphy, of course!

Christmas Decorations

You will need: cardboard, paint, modeling clay, candle, leaves, fir cones, glue, flour or icing sugar, glass baubles

Find a piece of thick card and cut out a circle or square. Paint it and put a large piece of clay in the centre. Stand a candle firmly in it.

Collect some leaves and berries and fir cones if you can find them. Paint them with glue and sprinkle with flour or icing sugar. Stick these into the clay. Add glass baubles and tinsel and maybe a ribbon bow. Try to cover up the clay with the leaves.

Put the decoration in the centre of the table, and light the candle for Christmas dinner. Watch that the candle does not burn low and set the decorations alight!

Paper Chains

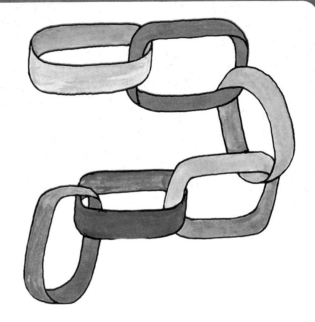

You will need: colored paper, glue
Cut some strips of colored paper and glue
the ends together, forming circles as shown
above. Link all the pieces of paper
together and drape across the room or the
Christmas tree. You can buy sticky strips
to make paper chains or paint some paper
yourself and use your own glue.

Painted Twigs

You will need: twigs, white or silver paint,
a pot, candies, aluminum foil
Find some twigs without leaves and paint
them white or silver all over. When they
are dry you can stand them in a pot and
hang pretty candies and circles of
aluminum foil on the twigs. You can
use some glass baubles and tinsel if there
are any left from the Christmas tree.

Paint some nutshells with silver and gold
paint and place them in a small bowl when
they are dry. You could add these to the
candle table decoration.

The New House

Pat and Dick lived in an old house. It was very small. It was not very good for playing in. Pat and Dick wished their house were bigger.

One day, their daddy called them. He said, "We are going to live in a big new house. Mummy and I think this house is too small. It was big enough when you were only babies, but not now."

Mummy said they should pack up their things. Pat looked at all her toys. She was really too old for some of them.

"I don't want to take these to our new house," she said.

"Well," said her mother, "it would be very nice to leave them. I know that a little baby is coming to live here when we have gone."

So Pat left her old toys behind. Dick left some, too. They were pleased about their new house. And they were sure the baby would be pleased with the toys. So everyone was happy!

How to Make the Spinners

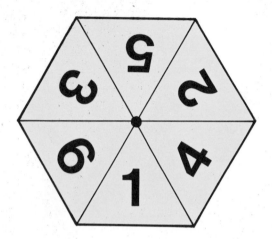

You will need: thin card, 4 rubber bands, tracing paper (or greaseproof paper), 2 fairly short pencils

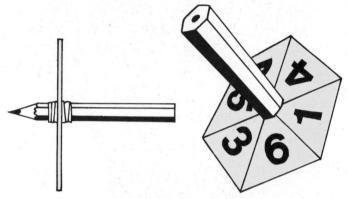

Trace the shape shown for the spinner, including the numbers. Trace down the shape onto thin card and cut out with scissors. Use a sharp point to make a hole in the center of the cut-out shape. Push the pencil carefully through until the card is about ½″ above the point. Wind an elastic band round the pencil above the card and another below, to hold the card in place. Now it is ready to use. When the spinner comes to rest, the number nearest to the table or desk surface is the number to use. The spinner that is used with the numbered spinner shown above for the *Around the World* game is made exactly the same way.

Trace the square shape on this page and trace down onto thin card.

Now make up the spinner exactly as you did the other one.

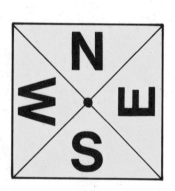

Answers

The Lost Pets

3 cats

1 dog   1 monkey

2 mice   1 snake

1 parrot   3 canaries

2 tortoises   1 rabbit

Treasure Hunt

scissors	hammer
pencil	drum
tea kettle	goldfish
carrot	clock
button	torch
telephone	saw

Stories and adaptations by the various
authors can be found on the following pages

Illustrations by the following artists